MOTIVATING VOLUNTEERS

IN THE
LOCAL CHURCH

ISBN: 083-411-4151

Printed in the
United States of America

Cover Design: Ted Ferguson

Unless otherwise indicated, all Scripture quotations are from the King James Version (KJV) of
the Bible.

Permission to quote from the following copyrighted versions of the Bible is acknowledged with
appreciation:

The *New American Standard Bible* (NASB), ©️ The Lockman Foundation, 1960, 1962, 1963, 1968,
1971, 1972, 1973, 1975, 1977.

The Holy Bible, New International Version (NIV), copyright ©️ 1973, 1978, 1984 by the International
Bible Society.

10   9   8   7   6   5   4   3   2   1

MOTIVATING VOLUNTEERS
IN THE
LOCAL CHURCH

by

LESLIE PARROTT

NAZARENE PUBLISHING HOUSE
KANSAS CITY, MISSOURI

To
Frank and Mabel Lay,
whose ministry of volunteering
is a continuing source of inspiration
to those who know them

Contents

Preface

Church life in some congregations reminds me of the athletic events in our local high school. A few weary, stressed-out players volunteer to keep the game alive while most of the people observe from the sidelines. The interpretive skill of those watching is honed in a critical commentary before, during, and after each game.

Have you ever noticed that these sideline observers are absolved of responsibility? They take no chances. They suffer no injuries. Usually they attend the games and gossip about every contingency (real or rumor) and make a comfortable donation to a special need such as the student drive for new uniforms. These observers don't experience guilt. They never know the fear of personal failure. But they also miss the exhilaration of involvement. They may experience the emotions of winning and losing, but only from a distance.

In intercollegiate games, there are rules about how many people can play. In church life there is no limit to the number of people who may be involved. That is what this book is about: How can we get more people involved as volunteers in the local church?

This is not a play book filled with diagrams on how to get the people out of the stands and into uniforms. Instead we will consider what the legendary basketball coach John Wooden called "getting back to basics."

Why do some church members volunteer and others do not? Why do some people with much-needed skills and resources bury their talents in their weekday jobs or in the maintenance of their lawns and leave the church to stretch the work of lesser-gifted people across more and more responsibilities? Why do some Christians use their hands while others only wring them in sanctified alarm?

This book offers no simplistic answers, but it does discuss (1) the scope and power of volunteers; (2) the problems of apathy and reluctance; and (3) a perspective on motivating volunteers in the local church.

There is a wealth of data on the general subject of volunteerism, but much of it is not applicable in the local church. The most helpful material I found was in doctoral dissertations that dealt with the fundamentals of why some church members volunteer and others don't.

I am indebted to Librarian Ruth Kinnersley for the computer searches and retrievals. I am further indebted to Jan Royal, a patient secretary who was not turned off on copy rewrites that must have seemed interminable during the two years of the project. I am glad for two excellent copyreaders, Charles Higgins and Yvonne Chalfant. And were it not for the help and encouragement from Dr. Bill Sullivan, the manuscript would never have been started or completed.

I have enjoyed this study because I believe the quality and spirit of volunteerism determines the level of local church effectiveness.

This book is divided into three parts: Part One deals with the overwhelming need for volunteers and the spiritual and numerical resources available to supply this need.

Part Two explores the fundamental area of motivation and emotion. What motivates people to volunteer? Why are many good people reluctant volunteers? What provides the staying power for volunteers?

And Part Three responds to the fundamental need for generating success in expanding the volunteer program of a local church.

Here's hoping for a quantum leap forward in the understanding of why some church members volunteer and others don't.

LESLIE PARROTT, Ph.D.
Olivet Nazarene University
January 1, 1991

Prologue
The Day Our Volunteers Quit

Everyone who goes to church knows volunteers are important. But those who depend on the week-by-week work of volunteers in the local congregation know they are indispensable. Their presence and power are indisputable. Without volunteers there would be no local church. As Jesus volunteered His life, the church is composed of those who, in a different way, volunteer their lives for His sake.

Let me tell you about a dream I had the other night. Or was it a nightmare?

I drove our family to church at the usual time. But I knew with one visual sweep of the premises that something was dreadfully wrong. My placid Sunday morning emotions were suddenly troubled. The chains that secured the lot against unauthorized all-night parking were still engaged. "What's wrong with our custodian?" I snarled. The vans that had been used on Saturday were still in the choice parking spaces closest to the church door. On Sunday, the custodian was supposed to move the vans to the unused area in the farthest corner of the lot and take down the chain that blocked the opening.

There were some good signs. The sanctuary lights were on. When I arrived at the entry, the latch on the large foyer door was unlocked as it should have been. And once inside, I noticed the heat was up and the place was tidy.

But the custodian was nowhere to be seen. His name echoed hollowly when I called for him. Immediately I phoned his home. His wife answered. She was still getting dressed for church, she said, but her husband, the custodian, had left early. In fact, a little earlier than usual. On the way out he had said something about being fed up with church members blaming him for all kinds of things that were not his job in the first place. "I am going to do what I'm paid to do, and nothing more," he'd said. "I'm through being a custodian who is expected to volunteer all kinds of time and services I don't get paid for!"

As I put down the phone, the implications of our custodian's comments began to sink in. He was staging a one-man walkout against all the volunteer services we expected from him just because he was the logical person to call on. Although it was an immature act on his part and very disruptive, I could see his point. In our church we expected the paid workers to volunteer far beyond their call of duty.

While my wife found the keys and went out to move the vans, I left the church office for the practice room to confer with the choir director. Our choir man was a wonderful person who made his living selling cars and gave his services as a volunteer song leader, choirmaster, producer of special events, director of small music groups, and colleague of the pastor in planning services of worship and evangelism. His wife played the piano and sang in a ladies trio. He was a key volunteer in the music of our church, and she was indispensable on the piano bench. We gave them a gift each Christmas and a part-time salary check each month. But actually, they were volunteers. They gave more money in the collection plates than the church board ever agreed to pay for their services. I was as guilty as the rest of the congregation in taking them for granted. After all, they were members. Shouldn't they volunteer their services? Without realizing it, our church had become insensitive to the time, energy, and talent these people volunteered each week.

On this unforgettable Sunday, the choir room was dark. No one was around. But on the door was a hastily scrawled note: "No choir today. Volunteers released."

I felt a sharp pain in my midsection, and my throat went dry. I caught my breath and asked the empty hallway: "What's going on? Have all the volunteers quit?" Then another aftershock hit me. I gasped as I realized the congregation was beginning to arrive, and the volunteer workers were not in their places.

In the Sunday School annex the story was the same. No lights. No movement. No volunteers. By now I saw children milling in the halls or sitting in their rooms hunched over like human question marks. I hurried to the Sunday School office to find the superintendent. He was not there. And neither were the statistical secretary and his assistant. Those two had requested these record-keeping jobs. I thought they were satisfied with the arrangement. And until now they had been faithful. But where were they today?

My first feeling of horror was turning into naked panic. "Where is everybody? ... Maybe there is something wrong with my watch! ... What is going on here?" Slowly, but irreversibly, the picture was developing in full color and distinct detail. "Could it be? ... I can't believe it! ... It must be so! ... The volunteers have quit!"

All the volunteers in our church had quit their jobs on the same Sunday. The volunteers were AWOL, absent without leave. The results of this volunteer rebellion were not simple inconvenience. They were devastating. The results were compounded because some volunteers had more than one major assignment.

All the things we took for granted on Sunday morning were missing. The church bulletins lay unattended on the foyer table because the greeters did not show. Worshipers found their own seats without ushers to help them. No one came forward to take an offering, so the men sat on their wallets, and the women closed their purses.

The organist played as usual because he was paid, but the pianist didn't because she was not. The nursery never opened, and so crying babies competed with the sounds of pastor's sermon. The elderly people who counted on volunteer rides to church were left in their homes, disappointed and confused. The scoutmaster canceled his Monday night meeting. All the small groups fell apart. The momentum of the church plummeted to zero.

I was considering resigning myself because of my impossible work load when I woke up in a cold sweat, sitting straight up in bed. I was trying to decide whether I had been dreaming when my wife said flatly from her pillow, "What's the matter with you?"

When my wife listened to the story of my dream about the rebellion of the church volunteers, she registered no sympathy. She laughed. "Your dream was a nightmare—and it should have been. You and most other pastors take volunteers for granted, when they're the most indispensable people you've got."

I

The Scope and Power
of Volunteers
in the Local Church

1

The Gallup Survey on Volunteers

Pastors and laymen recognize the importance of volunteers in local churches, but no one had ever done a definitive study on the scope and significance of church volunteers until 1988, when the Gallup organization was contracted by Independent Sector, a Washington, D.C.-based coalition of nonprofit organizations, and assigned the task.

The results of the Gallup survey have taken a lot of the guesswork out of evaluating the importance of church volunteers. The report leads us to several conclusions: (1) The services rendered by church volunteers dwarf contributions by volunteers in any other local organization. (2) People intent on identifying who makes the greatest difference in the volunteer service at the community level will, from now on, "need to acknowledge the pervasive work done at the community level by people who are members of America's religious bodies." (3) Churches are the places where the moral issues behind much volunteering are addressed. (4) Churches not only are interested in salvation but also are interested in organized neighborliness. And, (5) community churches, which are pluralistic in their theological view, will respond similarly in their concerns for both religious education and human needs. Nazarene, Baptist, Methodist, and all other churches are gatherings of people who believe somewhat differently but volunteer similarly.

The study by the Gallup organization had two purposes: (1) To explore the degree of influence these religious institutions have had on all volunteer services provided in our communities, and (2) to discover the ways that religious values motivate people to give their money and to volunteer their time to religious institutions and to other nonreligious, volunteer organizations in the community.

Under the terms in the United States Constitution for the separation of church and state, congregations became voluntary organizations on the day the nation was founded. There would be no national church supported by tax dollars. However, this voluntary nature of churches, free from governmental control, made it possible for any small gathering of worshipers to call themselves a church and any small group of churches to declare themselves a denomination. In 1988, when George Gallup did this baseline study of volunteerism among church members, there were approximately 100 denominations and nearly 300,000 churches and synagogues in America.

Mr. Gallup recognized a church to be a gathering of people who come together regularly for worship, fellowship, and service to their members and others. And all of these congregations, taken together, constitute the American mosaic of small, medium, and large congregations housed in properties that range from embarrassing to magnificent, from rented storefronts to nationally known cathedrals.

The Gallup people confirmed what many already believed. Most of these buildings are far from empty. In a recent survey, 60% of the adults reported they had attended church in the last six months. In a population of 250 millon, that's a lot of people in church on any given Sunday.

These congregations are not necessarily poor, although they often appear to take on more financial responsibilities than they can sustain. It is estimated that nearly 66% of all personal giving nationwide in 1989 went to local congregations. More than half of all Americans reported giving to their local church or synagogue. Also, nearly half of those who gave to their own congregation also gave to other charitable organizations. For the first time, this Gallup study makes it possible to get a profile of (1) the average congregation and (2) the average volunteer according to size of church.

A NATIONAL PROFILE

After doing a study of the telephone yellow pages, the Gallup people determined there were 294,271 congregations in the United States, with 70% of these located in metropolitan areas and 30% in nonmetropolitan areas. Most of the churches with less than 100 members are in the open country or in towns. Apparently it takes a large population area to grow a large church.

After 1900, the most active period for founding new congregations in the U.S.A. has been from 1951 to 1970. There are more churches in the north central states than in any other area, including the Southern Bible Belt. The smallest number of congregations was in New England.

Most of the congregations in America (42%) have memberships ranging from 100 to 399. For the purpose of our discussion we'll call these medium-size churches. About 23% have less than 100 members (small), while 35% have more than 400 members (large). No statistics were available on worship attendance.

The survey showed that 60% of the large churches were founded before 1930, and 40% of them were formed before 1900. Apparently, it takes time to grow a church. Only 6% of the large churches were founded since 1971, and only 25% of the small churches were founded before 1930.

As the writer of the Gallup report points out, "Religious institutions tend to be conservative because they engage in and preserve religious tradition." However, when Mr. Gallup asked the church members to rank themselves on a continuum from 1 to 10 as very conservative to liberal, 53% of the churches ranked themselves conservative or very conservative, while 40% ranked themselves as moderate or liberal. Only 7% did not know whether they were liberal or conservative. It is interesting to note, the older the congregation, the more likely it is to see itself as liberal. Most of these liberal churches were founded before 1900. Only 11% of the churches founded since 1971 saw themselves as liberal. Apparently, the conservatives are the most aggressive in founding churches.

On the matter of age, most church members, as expected, are in the working years of 18 to 64. The senior citizens and children constitute near equal numerical groups. (It seems a healthier statistic would have shown more children in church than senior citizens.)

In matters of race, 78% of the congregations were either all white or less than 10% ethnic. And, according to Mr. Gallup, only 2% of the churches in America are all black.

Nearly 160,000 congregations (54%) reported church growth in the last five years, while 26% were holding their own, and approximately 20% were decreasing in size.

WHAT VOLUNTEERS DO

Although the number and kinds of volunteer programs tend to increase with the size of the church, there are five easily identifiable programs most congregations provide for their members and communities. Most volunteers in local churches are involved in one or more of these five local church priorities.

At the top of church volunteer activity list are programs that relate to worship (choirs, ushers, readers, musicians, etc.) and religious or Christian education for both children and adults. In most Protestant churches, Christian education includes Sunday School. These volunteer services were reported by virtually 100% of the religious bodies in America.

The second priority in American churches is family counseling. Some form of volunteer family counseling is offered in almost 79% of American churches. Many predict this focus on family concerns will continue at least through the first decade of the next century.

Youth programs are the third priority among volunteers in American congregations. These programs include camping, recreation, and related activities. At 78%, youth programs are virtually tied with family counseling in proportion of churches involved.

Missionary work, international relief, or overseas compassionate ministries are important in 69% of the American religious organizations. However, size of a church makes a difference in the level of missionary involvement. Only 55% of the small churches supported these international programs, while 76% of the larger churches are involved.

The fifth priority among church volunteers is health programs. These volunteer services include donated time in hospitals, clinics, nursing homes, hospices, and the like.

PAID AND VOLUNTEER
CLERGY AND STAFF

The use of volunteers in local churches is universal. However, according to Gallup's survey, 37% of the 688,000 clergy who serve American congregations are volunteers. This means that more than a quarter of a million of the pastors in the U.S.A. preach without pay. Large churches average seven employees other than clergy. However, the idea of churches with only one clergyman is not yet out-of-date. Nearly 50% of the small churches have only one clergyman, while 42% of the medium churches (100 to 399 members) have but one pastor. Only 26% of the large churches reported one clergyman, while 17% of these churches reported three or more paid pastors.

Among congregations, 34% reported no paid people in the clergy's support system. In all churches, more than half (51%) reported no paid staff. This implies that these congregations are mobilized to volunteer for almost everything that is done in their churches including cleaning, secretarial service, and all church programs that serve their members and the community beyond.

Of the 1.6 million paid employees, not counting clergy, 352,000 are full-time staff members, 499,000 are part-time, and 306,000 are only paid nominally. My experience in local churches suggests that most people who serve in staff positions in local churches have a strong component of volunteer service factored into their assignment. Almost all church workers, including pastors and their wives, do more than they are paid to do. And many of the part-time employees probably give more to the church in donations than they are paid.

VOLUNTEERING YOUR TIME

Finally, the Gallup people found that 39% of the volunteers in very conservative churches gave more than 10 hours of service each month. In conservative and moderate churches the percentage was somewhat less, 31% and 27% respectively. And in liberal churches only 20% of the volunteers worked more than 10 hours each month. This means one in every two and a half church members in conservative and moderate congregations gives more than 10 hours in donated service each month. However, liberal churches need five members to produce one volunteer who works more than 10 hours in a month.

According to this study by the Gallup organization, more than 12 million clergy, staff members, and volunteers work a total of 301 million hours each month in the various programs of their local churches. Among all church workers, 85% are volunteers, 10% are lay employees, and 5% are clergy.

When it comes to the number of hours on the job in church work, clergy provide 39% of the total hours, paid employees 25%, and volunteers 36% of total hours worked. The average hours individuals volunteer per month does not vary much by size of congregation. Except for religious services, which are the first priority of churches, congregations devote most of their time and energy to programs in (1) religious education, (2) family services, (3) youth programs, (4) missionary and international compassionate ministries, and (5) health-related programs.

VOLUNTEERING YOUR MONEY

The funding of these American congregations is impressive. Total revenues for all congregations in the United States is more than $50 billion annually. The average 1988 revenues in congregations was $56,000 in small churches, $103,500 in medium churches, and $325,000 in larger congregations.

Overall, the average expenditure of all congregations was approximately $169,800. Of this total, $124,400 was spent on current operating costs. Another $29,000 is sent by the local congregations to support denominational and other programs outside their own church, and $14,100 is spent annually in construction and other capital costs including debt service.

Of the $8.4 billion given away by congregations, 65% is contributed to organizations within the denomination ($5.5 billion), 23% to organizations outside the denominations ($1.9 billion), and 12% ($1.0 billion) in direct assistance to individuals.

IN SUMMARY

As part of their religious beliefs, volunteers in local congregations engage in a variety of programs, designed to improve the lives of their members and their communities through religious education, human services, and institutional care in hospitals, clinics, and special homes for elderly.

1. Congregations have an international ministry as well as a community and regional concern. In all of these programs, volunteers do a significant amount of the work and give most of the money.

2. Nearly half of the individual donations to congregations are used to support a variety of programs that help people within their membership, communities, and beyond.

3. Congregations conduct much of their work through volunteers.

4. These members who volunteer spend nearly half of their time on worship and Christian education needs and the other half on human services and health- or hospital-related programs.

5. Congregations are funded 95% by voluntary giving though freewill collections and pledges.

FINAL OBSERVATIONS

Because volunteers in local churches are (1) universal as the study shows, and (2) indispensable as experience demonstrates, then what assumptions can we live by in planning volunteer programs in the local church?

The marriage of Christian belief with Christian service is much stronger than many people think. Almost as many congregations (93%) offer programs in human services and health areas as offer public worship services and classes in religious education. That is something to think about. The motivation to Christian service is universal among churches, and the variety of ways to volunteer are almost infinite.

Here are a few programs people fit into their voluntary service, although there are many more: (1) after-school programs, (2) battered women programs, (3) child abuse programs, (4) senior citizen programs, (5) preschool day-care programs, (6) family counseling, (7) foster care/parenting, (8) housing for senior citizens, (9) housing/shelter for the homeless, (10) meal services, (11) migrant/refugee programs, (12) tutoring, and (13) drug and alcohol abuse programs. Not all congregations have all these programs, but 41% of all churches in America have five or more of the above organized volunteer activities in place.

Churches are great centers for voluntary service. In a given month, more than 10 million laymen are volunteers in congregational service programs. Worship and Christian education accounts for almost half of the volunteer work in local churches. Gallup's study suggests that millions of Americans are first taught to volunteer in their local congregations, where 65% of all Americans hold membership.

People first develop the habit of systematic giving in the local congregation. The local church is the place where the gap between Christian commitment and Christian service is bridged. It is in the church that people learn to create the miracle of turning faith into action.

No doubt there will be other surveys in years to come, but this study done by the Gallup organization in 1988 has set the baseline and has established pervasive data on the fact that volunteers in the local congregation are indispensable.

2

A Nazarene Profile

After reading the Gallup report on volunteers in American churches, it seemed our discussion would be enhanced by a similar report on volunteers in the Church of the Nazarene. It will be helpful to see how the Nazarene profile on volunteers in local churches stacks up against numbers and percentages reported by Mr. George Gallup in his survey of all religious bodies in America. Also, there is need for additional information from Nazarene churches that will serve our purposes in better understanding the presence and the power of volunteers in local Nazarene congregations.

Information for this profile was received from two sources: the Church Growth Research Center in Kansas City, and a survey distributed to pastors in approximately 50% of the districts in the United States. The results of this data search have taken some of the guesswork out of where the denomination and its local congregations stand in effective volunteer programs. Even without computer numbers, several conclusions are clear.

Local Nazarene congregations are totally dependent on volunteers. As it came to me in the nightmare I reported in the Prologue, Nazarene churches would close down if the volunteers quit. They fill the pews, do the work, and pay the bills. Our volunteers deserve to be understood, and they will not be motivated by manipulation. The first step in motivating potential volunteers is to understand and appreciate their personal values and priorities.

Churches grow by expanding the number and increasing the effectiveness of their volunteers.

It is evident from the following study that Nazarenes are interested in both salvation and Christian service. Sanctifying grace prepares Nazarenes for the ministry of volunteerism. The larger the number of volunteers in the church, the greater the number of converts; and the greater the number of converts, the greater the number of potential volunteers. The corollary is obvious: Churches grow by expanding the number and increasing the effectiveness of their volunteers.

Nazarenes volunteer for humanitarian service in their communities with the same commitment they invest in their Christian service inside the church, such as singing in the choir, ushering, or teaching a Sunday School class.

The basic need among Nazarene churches is for more volunteers who have been adequately trained. John Wesley built the Methodist movement through lay volunteers who nurtured the people at the grass roots level. Nazarenes should study his methods!

A GENERAL PERSPECTIVE

With the computer assistance of Richard Houseal in the Church Growth Research Center in Kansas City, information based on data in the annual assembly minutes of the U.S.A. districts provides a numerical profile to compare and contrast with the national survey of all religious bodies done by Dr. George Gallup and his people. The Nazarene computer data also makes it possible to look at ourselves in ways not included in the Gallup report.

There were 5,157 congregations of Nazarenes in the United States in 1989, a small fraction of the 300,000 organized religious bodies reported by Gallup. According to Gallup, as we noted, 23% of churches have less than 100 members, 42% have memberships from 100 to 399, and the remainder, 35%, have more than 400 members.

The Church of the Nazarene does not match the national profile on sizes of congregations: Approximately 66% of the Nazarene congregations have less than 100 members, 31% have memberships ranging from 100 to 399, and just over 3% of the churches have more than 400 members.

These statistics mean that more than 29% of the Nazarenes in the U.S.A. belong to a church with less than 100 members, 52% belong to churches with 100 to 399 members, and only 19% belong to churches with more than 400 members.

The bulk of U.S.A. Nazarenes (52%) belong to the medium-size churches (100-399), even though 3% of the churches with more than 400 members account for more than 18% of the membership. It would seem the most fundamental kind of church work—leadership, facilities, and program—needs to be done in the small churches of under 100 members, where more than 29% of the U.S.A. Nazarenes are members. These small churches probably need (1) stronger, better-equipped leaders, (2) upgraded and more adequate facilities, and (3) more volunteer programs that are geared to the needs of their communities.

Another great challenge is to help the medium-size churches—100-399 members—burst out into the rarefied air of those thriving congregations with adequate leadership, updated facilities, and a variety of volunteer programs that are in tune with the times.

Further growth in the above-400 category will depend almost exclusively on the vision, commitment, and entrepreneurial spirit of its leadership.

George Gallup did not report on the ratios of membership to attendance in the national profile. However, in the Church of the Nazarene, attendance on Sunday morning is equal to almost 90% of membership. Nearly 37% of all people attending Nazarene churches on Sunday morning are in a church with less than 100 members, more than 50% are in churches with 100-399 members, and approximately 13% are in churches with more than 400 members.

Less than 60,000 people attend Nazarene churches with more than 400 members. Almost 300,000 attend middle-size churches, and more than 200,000 attend churches with less than 100 members. Apparently there is plenty of room for expanding volunteer programs in all Nazarene churches.

In the national survey, Dr. Gallup reported the greatest concentration of churches in the north central states. He did not define this area, so we can assume he used the United States Census tracts, which include Ohio, Indiana, Michigan, Illinois, and Wisconsin in the East Central States Census. The Olivet and Mount Vernon areas contain more than 28% of the Nazarene congregations. However, the South is more heavily churched with Nazarene congregations, since the Trevecca and Southern Nazarene University areas contain more than 30% of the churches. Among Nazarene regions, the smallest population of churches is in the region that includes Washington, Oregon, Idaho, Montana, and Wyoming.

Apparently George Gallup is right; it takes a long time to grow a strong church. Of the 167 Nazarene churches with more than 400 members, 60 are pre-World War II congregations, founded before 1940. And all but 7 were organized before 1970. Only 2 of these large churches are less than 20 years old.

However, age does not guarantee growth. Leadership and location must also be important factors. Of the 3,386 churches with less than 100 members, 2,585, or 76% of them, were organized before 1970. This means more than 3 out of 4 of these small churches are about the same size they have been through the years. And 963, or 28%, were founded before 1940.

The highest number of medium churches, 1,161, or 72%, were organized in the four decades between 1920 and 1960. Most of the medium-size churches have stacked up lots of years growing to their present strength. These churches are good candidates for expanding their growth patterns through more and better programs for volunteers.

The most fruitful decade in organizing new churches was the 1950s, when 942 congregations were begun. Since 1908, the Church of the Nazarene has organized 9,105 churches with 57%, or 5,157, still in existence.

Among the medium-size churches (100-399), 137, or only 9%, have been organized since 1970, and 887, or 55%, were organized before 1940.

As the general population, most Nazarenes are in the working years of 18-64. However, the proportion of children, 46% (crib to 18), to senior citizens, 18% (65 plus), in Nazarene congregations is an encouragement if these children can be nurtured and eventually integrated into adult church members.

In matters of race, 78% of the congregations surveyed by Mr. Gallup were either all white or less than 10% ethnic. According to him, only 2% of the churches in America are predominately black. However, among Nazarene churches, 92% of the congregations are predominately white, 2% black, and almost 3% Spanish. There are 23 categories of ethnic congregations in the Church of the Nazarene, but none of them has enough churches to equal 1% of the total number of U.S.A. Nazarene churches except the Blacks and Spanish.

Nearly 54% of the churches surveyed by Gallup enjoyed church growth in the last five years, while 26% were holding their own, and approximately 20% were decreasing.

If growth is indicated by a minimum of 5% membership increase in the Church of the Nazarene, 47% (2,340 churches) reported growth in the last five years. If a 5% loss in membership indicates a significant decrease, then 32% (1,596) of the Nazarene churches decreased in the last five years. And 21% (1,053) are holding their own.

Although the number and kinds of volunteer programs increase with the size of the church, there are easily identifiable programs most churches provide for their members and for their communities at large.

Virtually 100% of the congregations in the general population reported volunteer programs related to worship and religious education for children and adults. The same is true in the Church of the Nazarene. These programs include choirs, ushers, musicians, Sunday School teachers, nursery attendants, and other related volunteer groups.

The second priority in American churches is family counseling, offered by almost 79% of the churches in the general population. Among Nazarene churches, a family counseling program exists in 59% of the churches with more than 400 members, in 19% of the medium-size churches (100-399), and in 9% of the churches with less than 100 members. Nazarenes have a great amount of work to do in meeting the needs of troubled marriages and families.

George Gallup reported that missionary work or international relief was important in 69% of the congregations in America. Only 55% of the small churches supported these international programs, while 76% of the larger churches were involved. However, in the Church of the Nazarene, 93% of the congregations were committed to missionary and international compassionate ministries as demonstrated in funds paid on General Budget and Approved Specials. Only 357 churches, or 7%, gave nothing on the General Budget or Approved Specials.

PAID AND VOLUNTEER
CLERGY AND STAFF

In the general population, George Gallup reported 37% of the clergy who serve American congregations are unpaid. Among Nazarene churches, less than 10% of the clergy are volunteers, which means that approximately 500 Nazarene pastors preach, as it were, without pay. All other Nazarene pastors receive some amount of remuneration. It is also important to note that in the Church of the Nazarene, 28% of the pastors of churches under 100 members are bivocational.

According to Gallup, 51% of all churches reported no paid staff, while a mere 20% of Nazarene churches reported paid staff. This means that 80% of all Nazarene churches are mobilized to volunteer for almost everything that is done, including cleaning, secretarial services, and all church programs that serve the members and the community beyond.

My experience in local Nazarene churches suggest that most people who serve in staff positions in Nazarene congregations have a strong component of volunteer service factored into their assignment. Also, many pastors and their wives do more work than they are paid for. And many of the part-time employees probably give more to the church in donations than they are paid. It is fully apparent that volunteer service is indispensable in the congregations of the Church of the Nazarene.

A NAZARENE PROFILE
BY SIZE OF CHURCH

In the fall of 1989, a survey on volunteering in the Church of the Nazarene was distributed to more than 50% of the district superintendents, who asked pastors on their district to respond. Because of the large number of districts involved and the high proportion of churches represented in these district meetings, the information is considered a reliable summary of voluntary service in the denomination, as perceived by pastors.

In keeping with the Gallup study, the congregations of the Church of the Nazarene are divided into small, medium, and large as defined in his study.

Small congregations have from 1 to 99 members.

Medium congregations have from 100 to 399 members.

Large congregations have more than 400 members.

Although volunteer programs are consistent with the size of the church, the differences by size are often revealing.

There are reasons that families with growing children are tending toward larger churches with programs directed by trained leadership, and away from smaller churches who do not have the number of families necessary to provide all the volunteer programs people often consider important.

For instance, virtually all of the large churches have one or more full-time or part-time staff persons to help supervise and lead their volunteer programs. Every large church is expected to have a staff. However, only 60% of the medium-size churches have staff, and only 9% of the small churches.

A further complicating factor for small churches is the number of pastors who are bivocational, nearly 30%. Among these bivocational pastors, 18% reported their congregations did not pay them anything, and 52% reported their congregations paid less than 25% of their income. These pastors and congregations have their work cut out for them in a day of decreasing loyalty to a local church or even a denomination. Developing families today tend toward full-service churches with a variety of volunteer programs to choose from.

The number of volunteer (unpaid) clergy who help their pastor and serve their congregation in visitation and other ministries increases dramatically with the size of the church. Almost 60% of the large churches reported three or more unpaid clergy helpers. In the medium-size church, 53% of the pastors report volunteer clergy help, and among the small churches, 32% report volunteer help from clergy. Apparently, there are many retired or unassigned ministers who volunteer in local churches. This is a large and important volunteer group that will probably get larger as people live longer.

In the church office, the large churches average more than four volunteers per church, while the medium churches average a little more than one per church, and the small churches have church office help on the average of about one person for every two churches. No one knows how many of these volunteer office helpers are pastors' wives.

The number of volunteers in custodial and grounds keeping services has the same number and size of church differential as volunteers for office work. The large churches average 7.4 persons per church, the medium-size churches 2.7, and the small church 1.2.

For the results of this data from pastors, Nazarene churches have a large supply of people who volunteer for construction, remodeling, and painting: In the large churches, there are about 17 persons per church whom the pastor can call on for this kind of volunteering. In the medium-size church, the number drops to 5, and in the small church to slightly more than 1.

When it comes to care and maintenance of church vehicles, the large churches have an average of slightly over two people per church, and the medium churches one. In the small churches there is one volunteer for each three churches, on the average.

Among the small churches, 10% reported no supply of volunteers available for these specialized assignments including (1) office work, (2) custodial and grounds keeping, (3) construction, remodeling, and painting, and (4) the care and maintenance of church vehicles. Church-owned vehicles are one more scarce resource among smaller churches.

The proportions of paid and unpaid church musicians follows the same pattern: Some 94% of the large churches have a paid minister of music, while 6% count on volunteers. Among medium churches, 28% enjoy the services of a professional minister of music, while 94% of the small churches use volunteers or have no minister of music at all.

When it comes to the piano and organ, 82% of the large and 95% of the medium-size churches have volunteer accompanists, while 7% of the small churches do not have a piano. The ratios for voluntary organ players are about the same in the large and medium churches, while 28% of the small churches do not have an organ.

In the large churches, 53% have from 51 to 100 volunteer singers and musicians in their choirs, ensembles, and instrumental groups, and 18% report more than 100 volunteers in music. However, 22% of the small churches report no singers and musicians, while 42% of the medium churches have from 11 to 20 volunteers in their church music. This confirms the great difference that exists between the music resources in large churches and smaller ones.

Volunteers in worship-related assignments abound: The large churches average approximately 23 ushers and greeters per church, 6 sound and light people, 15 nursery attendants, and 9 others who read scripture, pray, or serve as counters. The medium churches have 10 ushers and greeters, nearly 3 sound and light people, and 8 in the nursery. In the small churches, there are approximately 3 ushers and greeters, almost no sound and light people, and an average of 1-5 nursery volunteers per church.

Without doubt, the Christian education area of the church uses more volunteer workers than any other program in the local church: In the large churches, 48% report the total number of teachers and workers from 21 to 40. In 44% of the medium churches, the total number of workers is from 11 to 20. And in the small churches, 57% report less than 10 workers in Sunday School. Since the size of a Sunday School is limited by the number of classes and volunteer teachers, there is room here for considerable growth.

Regardless of church size, the popularity of children's church is pervasive: Even in the small churches, 59% report an organized children's church.

The response to this question was interesting: "Not counting Sunday School, how many volunteers in your church work with junior high and high school young people in Sunday and weekday programs?" The answers were most definitive in the small and medium churches. In 23% of the small churches, there is no youth program, and in 61% the number of volunteers working with teens is from 1 to 5. The number of volunteers in youth work in the large church is spread evenly among the congregations, using groupings of 1-5, 6-10, 11-15, or 16-20 volunteers. In the large churches 35% reported 6-10 volunteers in their youth work. Apparently, there is no agreement among pastors in large churches on how many volunteers it takes to operate an adequate youth program. Or, it may be that large churches vary dramatically in the sizes of their youth programs.

Usually only large churches successfully maintain a singles ministry. Approximately 44% of the medium and 82% of the small churches reported no volunteers for this work. Among the large churches, 94% reported from one to five volunteers in their singles ministry.

A great many Nazarene churches are involving volunteers in a women's ministry. Among small churches, 65% have volunteers who minister to ladies. In the medium-size churches it's 89%. In the largest churches, 71% report more than five volunteers involved in women's ministry, with all large churches reporting volunteer programs in this area of service.

There was a wide difference in the voluntary programs for children such as Caravans, Scouts, and the like: Almost 60% of the large churches reported more than 20 volunteers working with children's programs, exclusive of Sunday School. Although 14% of the medium churches reported no volunteers for these children's activities, more than half reported from 1 to 10 volunteers working in this ministry. It is disappointing that 44% of the small churches did not report children's programs other than Sunday School. Of the 56% who did report volunteers in children's work, the number ranged from 1 to 5.

Senior citizens are a high priority in all but the small churches, where 65% reported they had no program for this age-group. In the medium churches, 81% reported the services of 1-5 volunteers with senior citizens, while all large churches reported from 1 to 10 volunteers in this area.

Besides the volunteer programs commonly found in most churches, there are specialized ministries that call for volunteers who can render vital services. Among large churches, 59% offer family counseling services, 53% conduct prison ministries, 47% conduct a preschool day-care center, 41% volunteer housing, food, and shelter for the homeless, 41% offer meal services to the elderly and sick, and 35% have tutoring available, 24% offer help for drug- and alcohol-dependent people, 24% have after-school programs, 12% have programs for battered women, 2.9% use volunteers in foster care and parenting, and 1.9% have migrant and refugee programs.

Among the medium churches, participation in these specialized programs drops dramatically. The highest involvement programs are 25% who offer housing, food, and shelter for the homeless, 21% who sponsor a preschool day-care center, 19% who offer family counseling, and 18% who volunteer meal services to homes.

Even the small churches try to offer specialized programs: 9% offer family counseling, 8% offer housing, food, or shelter to the homeless, 6% offer meal services to homes, and 5% have after-school programs.

In spite of the scope of volunteer programs offered by Nazarene churches, the proportions of total congregations involved in volunteering is not very encouraging. Among the large churches, 24% reported 20%-30% and 35% reported 30%-40% of their congregation involved in some kind of voluntary service. However, an average of 39 of these volunteers per church have two or more major assignments, which is both a commentary on the willingness of people to work and on the lack of dependable volunteers available. Of these volunteers, their pastor estimates 53% of them work from 1 to 5 hours per week and 41% from 6 to 10 hours.

In the medium-size churches, 42% of the churches report 20%-30% of their membership are volunteers, while an average of more than 11 volunteers per church hold more than two major assignments. Their pastors estimate 61% of them work from 1 to 5 hours per week. Another 25% work from 6 to 10 hours per week.

In the small churches 35% of the pastors estimate that 10%-20% of their membership is involved in volunteering. On an average, 3 people per congregation hold more than two major assignments. And 74% of them work from 1 to 5 hours per week.

When asked to report on their biggest problem in recruiting volunteers, the two primary reasons were the same in all three sizes of churches: "People think they are too busy," and "They lack a spiritual vision and commitment."

I have always believed the number of hours a pastor works has a healthy segment of volunteerism factored into it, including the seven-day-a-week responsibility and the "on call" factor 24 hours a day. By the pastors' own reports, it seems the smaller the church the less the work, and the larger the church, the more the work. In the large church, 53% of the pastors reported a workweek of more than 70 hours, and 47% reported a 60-70-hour week.

In the medium-size church, 49% reported a 60-70-hour week, with only 9% reporting more than 70 hours per week. Only 4% reported 40 hours or less per week.

In the small church, 48% of the pastors said they worked 40-60 hours per week, while 19% reported they worked less than 40 hours. This shorter workweek may reflect the bivocational pastor's need to work at a secular job. This study does not report on the number of working spouses who help support the ministry of their husbands or wives by augmenting their income. It appears there is a strong factor of volunteerism in the service of Nazarene pastors if the 40-hour week is considered standard. This long workweek may have prompted one pastor to write a wish on his paper, "That the many who do so little would share the load of the few who do so much."

VOLUNTEERING OUR MONEY

The funding of Nazarene churches in the United States is impressive. Total revenues by all Nazarene congregations in a recent year was more than $395,810,064, or an average of $76,752 per congregation. George Gallup reported that revenues in small churches nationally averaged $56,000; in medium churches, $103,500; and in large congregations, $325,000.

In the Church of the Nazarene small congregations of less than 100 members averaged $31,287 raised for all purposes. Medium-size churches (100-399) averaged $126,108. And the larger congregations, above 400 members, averaged $524,521. This differential in financial resources demonstrates a sharp contrast between the haves and the have-nots within the denomination. But it also demonstrates the high per capita giving of Nazarenes.

Nationally the average expenditure of all congregations in all denominations was $167,700. Of this total $124,000, or 74%, was spent on current operating costs.

In the Church of the Nazarene, the average expenditure of all congregations in 1989 was $77,205. Of this total, $16,983 was spent on salaries and benefits. Nazarene churches averaged another $10,919 on indebtedness plus another $34,586 spent on other local budget concerns. This means on average $62,488, or 81% of all income, was spent locally. Among all Nazarene churches, $2,217, or 3% of all money raised, was given to the colleges and universities through an education budget, and to the seminary and Bible college beyond the basic support they receive through the General Budget. On an average, Nazarene churches paid $3,841, or 5%, on district expense. And finally, the general church received an average of $8,659 per church, which is equal to 11% of average money raised for all purposes.

It is obvious that churches with large debt service are severely hampered in their funding of service to others, including education, district, and general causes.

Of the $8.4 billion given away by all congregations in the United States, 65% is contributed to organizations within the denominations, 23% sent to organizations outside the denominations, and 12% in direct assistance to individuals. In the Church of the Nazarene, less than 1% of money received went to causes outside the denomination.

SUMMARY THOUGHTS

Below is a sampling from the profile of volunteerism in the Church of the Nazarene, along with some preliminary conclusions.

1. There is a sharp distinction between the have-nots (66% of the churches, with less than 100 members), and the haves (3% of the churches, with more than 400 members). If the church were poor, rich, or middle class as people are, the medium church (100-399) is the great middle class among Nazarene congregations.

2. It seems the most promising resource for expanding volunteer programs and increasing growth is this great middle class, the medium churches of 100-399 members. They have enough momentum to survive, enough strength to assure reasonable good health, but not enough energy to break out into the sunshine of a thriving congregation with the resources in personnel and finances to mount a full-orbed program of services for their people and the people they could attract.

3. The biggest single inhibitor to good financial health is an overburden of debt with a payback schedule that is too heavy to take in stride while implementing an expanded volunteer program with the necessary professional supervision and leadership that come with a good staff. This predicament makes nonpayment of education, district, and general budgets very tempting.

4. The church cannot be all things to all people. It takes courage to abandon programs that cannot be funded or

staffed in favor of a few well-directed volunteer programs that are most likely to expand growth of the congregation.

5. Several of the chapters in this book will speak to the twin problems most pastors found in trying to recruit volunteers: "People are too busy," and "They do not see the vision and make the commitment." People are no busier than they choose to be. And the pulpit is the best podium for helping people see the vision and make the commitment.

6. Retaining volunteers is often more difficult than recruiting them. Therefore, recruitment and training are the opposite sides of the same coin in voluntary service.

II

Facing the Problems
of Apathy
and Reluctance

3

Working with Reluctant Volunteers

Grandpa, in *The Cold Sassy Tree,* taught his grandson that "life is like pouring water into a Coca-Cola bottle. If you're afraid, it's hard to get it in." Pastors and lay leaders who depend on volunteers know many people do not participate because they are afraid. And fear in the mind of a potential volunteer turns to apathy.

Apathetic bystanders are often loyal church members whose regular presence in the worship services would be missed if they suddenly disappeared. But in spite of their good qualities, they just don't get deeply involved. They are reluctant to volunteer. They may be afraid of getting hurt, afraid of failure, or afraid of new relationships.

In a 1975 study by Savage, this reluctance to volunteer was identified and called the 80/20 principle, 80% of the work done by 20% of the people. This 80/20 principle has been researched, validated, and often quoted by social psychologists who study ratios of potential participation to actual involvement in volunteerism. Unfortunately, the 80/20 principle is validated in many churches where the volunteers continue to be a conspicuous minority.

Why do some church members become paragons of model volunteers who can be counted on year after year, while other church members are in and out of lay service, making promises of loyalty like Peter did to Jesus and then denying their commitment when the pressure is turned on?

This question of the reluctant volunteer has plagued a long line of pastors and lay leaders who have suffered over the lack of workers in local churches. Apathy has been the object of much research and study by social psychologists, philosophers, and theologians, who have probed the mind and spirit to find the roots of reluctance. The problem of apathy and reluctance is faced every week by lay commentators in the church parking lot who talk to each other about why it is always difficult to get enough sponsors for the teen work, teachers for the Sunday School, and volunteers to clean the churchyard and mow the lawn. Whether we study the reluctant volunteer at the operational level—getting enough workers for next week's event—or the deeper motivational level of theologians, philosophers, and psychologists, the problem persists. Why is it that some people volunteer and others don't?

THE MURDER OF KITTY GENOVESE

On an early spring morning in 1964, when daylight was just beginning to illuminate the concrete canyons of New York City, Kitty Genovese was walking alone, on her way home from an all-night job. En route she fell victim to a thief who was also a killer.

When her shrieks and screams for help began waking people in this respectable New York neighborhood, potential volunteers who could help save her from the assailant looked apathetically out their windows, afraid to get involved. A later study reported a minimum of 38 people watched from well-protected viewpoints above the street level where the assault was taking place.

To their credit, some bystanders opened their windows and yelled for the man, who was viciously stabbing Kitty Genovese, to go away. Leaving her on the sidewalk bleeding and brutally beaten, the man did go away, but only for a short time. He returned to renew his stabbing attack. Once more there was a commotion, and the robber fled. But he returned a third time to complete the murder.

Not one of the 38 spectators came to Kitty's defense or even called the police until after she was dead. The person who did report the crime first phoned a friend for advice on whether or not to get involved.

The Kitty Genovese murder in the sight of 38 witnesses who failed to volunteer help propelled a national outcry. The media branded the incident a "national disgrace" and editorialized on "the dehumanization of American society." Commentators called the case an indication of "moral callousness" in America. They wrote and spoke about our national "loss of human concern and compassion," and demonstrated, through spectacular pictures from other cities, that "the serious moral flaw" in America's national fiber was not restricted to New York City.

Although the media has reported many other similar events of thieving and violence in the midst of apathetic witnesses who did nothing to help the victim, no crime has focused the attention of social psychologists more on this one aspect of volunteerism than the murder of Kitty Genovese. More than 1,000 articles and books have been written to explain bystander apathy. If we are attacked, will those who are witnesses just stand around, or will they volunteer to defend us, even at their own risk? This is what some psychologists call our "primordial nightmare."

VOLUNTEERISM ON THE
ROAD TO JERICHO

Jesus described a real-life Palestinian situation that contains several of the factors in the assault on Kitty Genovese. Jesus said, "A certain man went down from Jerusalem to Jericho, and fell among thieves, which stripped him of his raiment, and wounded him, and departed, leaving him half dead" (Luke 10:30).

In the days of Jesus, the highway from Jerusalem to Jericho was 25 miles of twisting, turning road made for camel drivers, pedestrians, and men who rode little burros laden with goods. At either end of this ancient road were the cities of Jericho or Jerusalem. Jericho was that bustling regional city where Zacchaeus collected the Roman taxes. Jerusalem was the center of religious government where the top agenda was Temple politics. To make matters worse, terrain between Jerusalem and Jericho dropped a full 2,500 feet, which meant the burros were difficult to control and could be easily spooked by violent thugs who inhabited this barren strip.

The road to Jericho was an ideal setting for bandits who thrived by robbing traveling people who could not defend themselves when outnumbered by their assailants. Most people on this road traveled in caravans as did Mary, Joseph, and Jesus on their pilgrimage to Jerusalem some 18 years earlier. But in Jesus' story, the victim was apparently alone, well possessed with salable goods, and defenseless against the violence of a thieving gang.

While the band of brigands was off in some concealed cave in the hills, counting their loot, Jesus told what happened next. Three men came by while the poor victim still lay naked in his own blood, helpless and dying.

The first man who happened by was a member of the clergy. How fortunate; a man of God. How unfortunate; he was in a hurry. He may have been on a tight schedule, rushing to deliver a spiritual message that evening in Jericho. Or, if he had been going in the reverse direction, up the mountain toward Jerusalem, he might have been hurrying to a board meeting in General Headquarters near the Temple. God knows how eager priests were to get headquarters approval for their projects. Furthermore, a priest was the kind of religious man who, by profession, was most interested in the policies that made organized religion run smoothly. With him, the development of policies was more challenging, and even more important, than cases. The individual case of one robbery victim could never compete with the urgency of policy-making meetings. With these first-century priests, policies were more important than people. The schedule was more important than the person. To say the least, the priest couldn't afford to interrupt his important travel plans by attending the needs of one bleeding, unknown, helpless man. He was just too busy and probably too important to volunteer.

Next on the scene, according to Jesus' account, was a Levite, not a member of the priesthood but a significant person in the supporting staff. He did better than the priest because he stopped and examined the hurting victim. It was apparent to the Levite that the assaulted traveler did need help. But it was not apparent to him why the traveler ever allowed himself to get into his predicament in the first place. "When will these people ever learn?" he said pompously. "If he had only sat in on my time management seminar, I would have warned him about the treachery of business travel to Jericho. He should have known to travel in a group, or in the early morning when the ruffians are still asleep."

Jesus said, "The Levite . . . passed by on the other side" (v. 32). Unless you plan on volunteering when you're needed, don't come too close to human need. From the other side of the road, it is harder to see the face of a dying man. Looking on from a distance gives space for an unseen screen to keep the needs of mankind from becoming personal. This Levite had no trouble loving mankind; it was getting too close to people that troubled him. If you don't want to volunteer, keep your distance.

Finally, to the glory of God and the saving of the helpless victim, a Samaritan came by. When he saw the man, the Samaritan stopped, slid off the back of the little burro he was riding, and performed a series of immediate acts of compassion. Turn to Luke 10:34 and count the good things this Samaritan did:

The Samaritan "went to him." There was none of this "other side of the road" compassion with him. As a willing volunteer, he was drawn to the man with a need, like slivers of steel are drawn to a magnet. He did not volunteer because all his friends did. He volunteered because he had cultivated a willing heart.

The Samaritan "bound up his wounds." He provided the healing of oil and wine poured lovingly into the burning cuts. It is easier to talk about problems than it is to provide solutions. It is easier to talk about who did wrong than it is to start doing something to heal the situation. But the Samaritan turned his immediate attention to the healing process.

The Samaritan "set him on his own beast." This means he voluntarily inconvenienced himself. He temporarily gave up his own means of transportation. He probably made himself late to his next appointment. His schedule was not as important as a hurting stranger. There is no such thing as a willing hand without a sacrificial heart. They go together like love and forgiveness.

The Samaritan "brought him to an inn." The Samaritan was probably under as much pressure of time as either the priest or Levite. But he arranged for the continuing help the victim needed, the kinds of help he could not personally stay to give. He did not make a quick fix gesture designed to get the immediate guilt feeling off his back. The Samaritan took time to make arrangements for continuing help to this unknown person he found dying in the road.

The Samaritan "took out two pence" (v. 35). This was a day's pay! And he left it with the innkeeper to cover unspecified costs. Willing volunteers seldom think about counting the cost before they become involved with people who need them. In fact, it is true in local churches that those who volunteer the most time and energy often give the most money to make things go. Don't count on financing the church with people who, like the priest, are too busy to volunteer, or people who, like the Levite, keep a safe distance. Reluctant volunteers and apathetic bystanders don't have a high level of per capita giving.

And finally, the Samaritan made arrangements to follow up on the poor victim when he came back through Jericho on his return journey. "When I come again, I will repay thee" (v. 35). The will to help begets Christian involvement, and Christian involvement begets commitment, which always leads to follow-up.

The Samaritan didn't have any more knowledge about looking after robbery victims than either the priest or the Levite. He wasn't more skilled for the task. The difference between them and him was in his heart. "When he saw him, he had compassion on him" (v. 33). And for the Samaritan, compassion meant action.

Actually the Samaritan was not a likely volunteer. He could easily have been a reluctant bystander, and no one would have blamed him. He was a long way from home, where no one would have known what he did or did not do. The Samaritan was not under any peer pressure. Many people volunteer because their friends do. Group pressure makes them feel guilty if they don't volunteer. They do the good thing to insure themselves against social chastisement if they don't. But with the Samaritan, there was none of this kind of pressure. If he had not volunteered, no one would have known it.

The Samaritan was a traveling man who knew the ravages of the road. Highway tragedies are common sights to veteran travelers. Like a bypasser at a wreck on the interstate, the Samaritan could have looked on the scene with flashes of emotion that faded into apathy through the rearview mirror. He could have salved his guilt with a thought like, I'm sure the emergency vehicles will be here soon, and they are equipped to help him better than I am. I haven't even had a first aid course. As a traveling man, he could have seen this brutally beaten man as a highway statistic and ignored him as a person. No one would have known the difference.

The Samaritan was from people who did not have a good religious reputation. Samaritans were despised by Jews. The victim lying in his own blood probably had the anti-Samaritan bias common among all Jewish people. Samaritans were the odd people out. They were the visible, easily identified minority. Years later, when Philip led a great revival among the Samaritans, his ministry shocked all the Christians in Jerusalem. They sent their two best leaders, Peter and John, to check on matters and report back to headquarters. If the good Samaritan had passed by the Jewish victim on the road between Jerusalem and Jericho, no one would have been surprised. Jews and Samaritans didn't like each other. The Samaritan's unlikely status as a willing volunteer in the circumstances of this robbery and beating is what makes this story unforgettable. He was not a likely volunteer, especially on a Jewish highway frequented by Jewish travelers.

There is one last fact about Jesus' story of the good Samaritan; the 80/20 principle was at work in the ancient world where Jesus lived, just as it is today. In fact, the ratio of willing volunteers to reluctant bystanders on the road to Jericho was one in three, which is a little better than the 80/20 principle Savage found in his study. Three men saw the helpless victim, and only one stopped to volunteer help. I wonder if one volunteer for every three church members is about normal for most churches today. What the Lord needs is a few more good Samaritans.

THE PRINCETON STUDY

John Darley and Daniel Batson conducted a study to test religiosity as a motivator in helping the unfortunate. The dynamics of the research were a setup, but its results confirmed the fact that religiosity does not motivate pro-active behavior toward hurting people.

The study was done on students at Princeton Theological Seminary. A confederate in the experiment was placed, slumping and immobile, in an alleyway, coughing and groaning with his head down and his eyes closed. It did not matter to the seminarians who walked around the man in the corridor that they were on their way to class where some of them would give academic reports on Jesus' story of the good Samaritan. They passed by the victim because they were late for class or because they were sure others would help him. One seminarian actually stepped over the victim in an effort to gain a second or two on the clock.

The results of this study are not reported here as a put-down on seminary students at Princeton. The report is included here because it helps confirm the fact that we can be very religious and still fail to have the motivation to volunteer our help. The pressure of life conspires to make each of us a reluctant bystander.

BYSTANDER RESEARCH

A review of bystander research includes some interesting observations:

There are some people who are more disposed than others to help people in distress, even at high personal cost and considerable risk to themselves. And there are other people who have a lifelong pattern of passing by on the other side of the road.

A sympathetic attitude toward people in general is a major factor in most volunteering. It is hard to offer sacrificial help if you have no feeling for the general welfare of all people who are hurting.

Childhood experiences in helping others seem to be important among adults who volunteer. Many adult volunteers had parents who also volunteered.

Good Samaritans seem to possess a spirit of adventure and unconventionality in a greater degree than apathetic bystanders. The mother of President Jimmy Carter combined courage with adventure when she joined the Peace Corps after she was past 60 years of age.

People who usually volunteer their help feel guilty when they do not. Although guilt as motivation will be discussed in another chapter, it is important to say there is an important difference between (a) serving to get rid of guilt and (b) feeling guilty when you don't serve. The people who take a church job because they feel guilty will likely forsake the job when their guilt is relieved. The people who love to sing in the church choir will feel depressed when forced to drop out because they are missing the opportunity to serve, which had been a fulfilling experience in their life.

A RIVER OF LOVE

Bystander research does not satisfy all the questions among pastors and lay leaders on why some friendly, decent, well-behaved church members systematically pass by their opportunities to serve through volunteering their time and energy. Yet, the effectiveness of a congregation depends on the willingness of people to work with one another and share the benefits of this voluntary service with each other.

I am amazed at the number of "one another" sayings in Scripture. It is questionable whether a gathering of Christians could endure as a congregation unless church members are willing to assume responsibility for each other's welfare and to volunteer in helpful ways.

There is a river of Christian love that must become the mainstream of the congregation, or the church dies of social stagnation. This love within the congregation may express itself in a variety of ways:

Members are helpful to one another when sympathy expresses itself in the sorrow or sadness of another church member's hard times. Organized neighborliness is often an orderly expression of the level of sympathy felt toward one another in the congregation.

Love expresses itself in general through a spirit of common cooperativeness. Cooperation, or "going along," implies a willingness to work with others whether or not we always agree on everything. Cooperation is a mind-set. When this cooperative way of thinking is the predominate attitude in the church, the river of love becomes a mainstream through the congregation.

Mercy and forgiveness in an assembly of Christians imply a willingness to let people be themselves, including all their faults and failures and even their irritating ways. Most of us need mercy because we can't survive on justice. If we got what we deserved, we wouldn't even be members in the family of God. There is no love without mercy and forgiveness.

Loving sacrifice implies willingness to do without and accept risks for the sake of others. Not all the stories of rescue are as dramatic as the saga of the McClure baby who fell into a backyard well in Midland, Tex. But in every church there are situations that will never be resolved unless someone is willing to do something dramatic, even at great personal cost and inconvenience, for the sake of others. The unconditional factor in Christian love makes it possible to serve without expecting external reward; or does it? Ideally we volunteer without expecting rewards, but in reality, our voluntary spirit often turns to apathy if there is no recognition and reward.

ALTRUISM AND AGAPE

When social psychologists study altruism, which is their word for their unconditional love *(agape),* they usually come to some conclusions on motivation that are more realistic than idealistic:

People are motivated toward loving behavior while consciously or unconsciously expecting personal gratification. The couple who volunteer to decorate the church for Christmas had better receive public and private expressions of approval and appreciation, or they will be hard to recruit for the same job next year. Volunteers may expect material benefits, social approval, honor, or simply a sense of well-being from doing a good job. Negatively they may expect freedom from guilt. The belief in God's blessings and His punishments is a strong factor in much Christian motivation. Since motivation cannot be seen and only inferred from people's behavior, Christians, like all other people, persistently judge the motives of others, rightly or wrongly. But one fact is sure: Everyone has a motive for whatever they do. And the social psychologists believe that this motive meets the personal need of the volunteer more than the need of someone else. To say the least, motives are almost always mixed. "I am willing to meet your need if, in doing so, I also meet my own need." However, humanist social scientists believe the balance between the needs of the volunteer and the benefactor must tilt in favor of the volunteer. With Christ as our Model, Christians like to think of service to others as unselfish.

Church members also behave in loving ways because of self-rewards. Through the stages of our moral development, we internalize certain standards of behavior, which we experience as obligations and responsibilities. We feel good about ourselves when we behave in accordance with our inward standards and principles, and bad when we do not. When we do what we see as right, we reward ourselves with feelings of self-esteem; and when we compromise what we believe is right, we experience feelings of guilt. We reward ourselves for doing right, and we punish ourselves for doing wrong. It is a psychologically dangerous thing to deviate from our own internalized standards.

Many students of motivation single out empathy as the third motivating factor in loving behavior. We have empathy when we can stand in someone else's shoes, distill events through their emotions, and perceive through their mind-set. I have empathy with you when I can see, and feel, and structure events as you do. This is why it takes a married woman to empathize with a prospective bride, or a father who has walked through the teen years with a rebellious son to understand another man whose son has turned against him. The good Samaritan had empathy, while the priest and Levite satisfied themselves with a low level of sympathy. Empathy leads us to assume the perspective of another and see the world as he sees it. Empathy is the counselor's most powerful tool. Empathy reduces, or eliminates, the tendency to criticize. If I can understand how you think, I can also understand why you feel the way you feel. Bystanders who are led by the Holy Spirit to learn empathy are transformed into good volunteers. Christians who have a great sense of empathy often serve with an inspiring sense of mission.

Social psychologists also believe that people who are good Samaritans in one situation may not be in another. The results of studies focused on specific traits of character that are supposed to explain consistent good Samaritan behavior in a variety of settings have been discouraging.

For instance, it is estimated that 200,000 Jews were saved by non-Jewish rescuers during Hitler's reign of terror. Studies of these non-Jewish persons who helped Jews escape Nazi Germany found that rescuers tended to be adventurous, enjoy living with a margin of danger, and often possessed a special skill specifically needed for the rescue, such as the ability to forge passports or ski the mountain passes of the Alps. But in another situation that called for less exposure to danger and less specific skill, these same people became bystanders or reluctant volunteers. A good Samaritan is not necessarily a good Samaritan in every situation that calls for a volunteer.

The researchers also learned that many people became involved in the Jewish rescue work with a small beginning commitment, such as the promise to protect a Jew for a night or two. Taking the first step led the volunteer to see themselves differently and ultimately motivated a much deeper and sometimes irreversible commitment to help save Jews. Raoul Wallenberg, the Swedish diplomat who used his position to save hundreds of Hungarian Jews, started by saving a Hungarian-Jewish business partner. Soon he was manufacturing passes that made Jews eligible for Swedish citizenship and hence beyond the authority of their German captors. As Wallenberg's commitment grew, he exposed himself to greater and greater risk until he was finally providing passes for Jews standing in lines waiting for deportation trains.

A fifth factor scholars have identified in good Samaritan behavior is moods. There is meaning in moods. We are most likely to volunteer our help during our good moods. Generosity is fostered by positive feelings. Good fortune, such as receiving an unexpected gift, makes us more generous with our time and money than being depressed by unpaid bills. Sunny days improve our moods. One group of researchers found that people in good moods are more likely to retrieve positive pictures from their memory other than negative ones. This is why a church with a positive atmosphere and a happy congregation is likely to enjoy a high rate of volunteerism. Positive church experiences create a congregational mood that fosters volunteerism. Positive people with positive pastors reinforce each other.

Social scientists believe people volunteer more readily when they have received a clear, positive challenge to serve. Many pastors and lay leaders have pondered the 80/20 principle and wondered why so many people do not readily volunteer in the church. One reason is that the need is not made clear.

Before bystanders decide to volunteer, they consciously or unconsciously take several preliminary steps. (1) They become aware of the need. (2) They interpret the importance of the need. And, (3) they decide whether or not it is their responsibility to volunteer help. Before I sing in the choir, teach a class, or tutor students, I must have my awareness of the need increased. I must decide the need is really important. And I must see myself with the responsibility to step forward and volunteer to meet the need.

In the church's need for volunteers, there may be a breakdown at any one of the above points. (1) A church member may not be aware of the need. The announcement was unclear or its message was lost in the humorous character of the skit that was intended to heighten awareness. (2) A church member may fail to interpret the importance of the need. Or, (3) the church member may fail to feel any personal responsibility. If there is a breakdown in any one of these preliminary steps, the church member will remove himself from the volunteering process and leave the pastor frustrated about congregational apathy. When this breakdown occurs, the potential volunteer becomes one more statistic on the wrong side of the 80/20 equation.

Even if the church member consciously or unconsciously sorts out the first three steps—awareness, importance, and responsibility—there are two more steps to be made before joining the line of volunteers. (4) The potential volunteer asks, "Will what I can do make a difference?" And (5) "How do I go about responding to this need for volunteers? Do I contact the pastor, just show up, or inquire around?" If someone is uncertain about how to volunteer, he may not volunteer at all.

Church members are more likely to volunteer for a need that is a clear challenge than one that is ambiguous. However, when church members are uncertain about the call for volunteers, they may still step forward to help, but for different reasons: (1) A reluctant bystander may watch the responses of others, particularly those whose opinions he cares about, and wait to see what these persons do. If their friends stand up to be counted, they may join them. We take cues from the behavior of our friends and those whose opinions we care about. (2) Our concern about how our fellow church members will evaluate us may increase or inhibit our potential for volunteering. Also, (3) church members may volunteer if they feel their specific help is needed, whether or not they have much awareness of the need. When the pool of potential volunteers is large, the level of personal responsibility is low. If I'm one of the few options the pastor has, my feelings of personal responsibility will likely be increased.

This phenomenon of potential surplus volunteers was probably a factor in the murder of Kitty Genovese because the 38 "bystanders" were aware others were watching and assumed someone else would do something. Social psychologists have a name for the phenomena of reduced personal feelings of responsibility in the face of "surplus" helpers. It's called the Bystander Effect.

When bystanders are cohesive in the local church, as people who know one another and have ties to one another, they may appear as a power block when actually they are only waiting for each other's responses to the call for help. None of us likes the threatening emotion of feeling alone. If we volunteer, we want others to volunteer also.

This brings us to the tension between love and guilt as motivators for Christian service. How much of our church volunteering is done out of love and how much is done out of guilt? Do we pay our tithe because we love God or because we feel guilty if we don't? Do we cooperate in the Sunday School visitation program because we love lost souls or because we would feel bad for failing to support the pastor? Do we sing in the choir in recognition of God's gift of a melodic voice or for the recognition we get for "helping out" and the applause of the congregation when our singing inspires them?

People seldom do anything because of one single motive. We volunteer for multiple reasons. We volunteer at different levels and in different ways. And in all instances we are dominated by feelings of love and guilt that motivate us accordingly.

Whatever Happened to the Volunteers?

Christian evangelism across the Roman Empire was primarily the work of volunteers. Wherever Christians migrated, people were led to Christ and accepted Him as Lord. Communities were changed, not by professional evangelists or robed officials of the church, but by committed laymen. They volunteered their homes as gathering places for believers. They worked at a trade for a living but focused their lives on serving Christ. They made tents, presided over a potter's wheel, managed a shop, or served as carpenters and stonemasons. Many of them were slaves. All of them were volunteers.

Edward Gibbon, in his book *The Decline and Fall of the Roman Empire,* has a classic chapter on what caused the rapid spread of Christianity across the Roman Empire in a hostile, inhospitable environment. He said, "It became the most sacred duty of the new convert to diffuse among his friends and relations the inestimable blessing which he had received" (2:7).

John R. Mott, commenting on this fiery phenomenon of spiritual enthusiasm among members in the Early

Church, said, "Wherever Christianity spread, families were converted, not just by Peter and Paul but by everyone. It was the work of the amateur" (Mott, quoted in Green, *Called to Serve,* 2-3).

These volunteers in the Early Church had nothing to offer but their willingness to serve. Many of these Christians were slaves without rights of citizenship, but they volunteered anyway. They could talk about Christ with other slaves and sometimes with their masters. Their only tools were (1) *faith in Christ,* which was demonstrated by a purity of life for which they would rather die than compromise, and (2) *an unbeatable goodwill,* which the New Testament writers called *agape* or unconditional Christian love.

The question today is: Whatever happened to the volunteers?

At a time when volunteerism is on the national agenda, the number of volunteers in the church is falling short of the needs to be met. According to a recent story in the *New York Times* by Peter Steinfels, volunteers have been leaving the church in unprecedented numbers. The United Methodist church dropped 18% in its membership between 1965 and 1987. Other churches have seen a more drastic decline: The Presbyterians lost 25%, the Episcopalians 27%, the United Church of Christ 20%, and the Disciples of Christ 42%. Tithes, offerings, and other gifts in the mainline churches have declined a whopping 53% since 1965 when adjusted for inflation.

However, besides the Catholics, Mormons, and Seventh-Day Adventists, who enjoyed their usual numerical increases, Steinfels reported on a group of small, conservative denominations who enjoyed "significant increases" in membership. They include (1) Christian and Missionary Alliance with a 2.3% increase, (2) Church of God, Anderson, up 5.2%, (3) Church of the Nazarene up 2.4%, (4) Free Methodists up 2.2%, and (5) Four Square Gospel Church up 3.2%.

Unfortunately these five denominations with growth, which the *New York Times* calls "significant," only total

1,351,132 in membership, which is 1 million less members than there are Catholics in the archdioceses of Chicago. Or to put it another way, these conservative denominations represent less than 1% of the 143,830,806 Americans who belong to a church or synagogue.

In addition to the volunteers who have left the church since 1965, there is another big problem that needs to be addressed: Many pastors report significant decreases in the proportion of church members who are willing to volunteer. They may be busy, tired, distracted, or unchallenged, but the consequences are the same. Church members today don't volunteer as their parents did. Many are waiting passively for the announcement of one more seminar on how the church should identify and meet the needs of its members. For these Christians, the inner light of loving service is either burning low or is extinguished. They fail to see the connection between Christian service and spiritual well-being. These uninvolved members suffer from loss of stamina that comes from sitting on their hands year after year. This sluggish condition in the spiritual bloodstream is difficult to cure. In many cases, hardening of the spiritual arteries becomes irreversible. As far as life in the church is concerned, a passionate wringing of the hands is no more helpful than sitting on them. Spiritual alarmists are just that: spiritual alarmists. Lifting our voices is not a substitute for using our hands. Voluntary service is the best, if not the only, antidote to spiritual apathy in the local church.

THE PREACHER WITH CHARISMA

For one thing, we have gone through an era that has featured the popular charismatic preacher as the ultimate answer to church growth. At home on the couch watching Sunday morning Christian television, or in church with upholstered pews, the church people are deserting their traditional commitments in favor of the gifted speaker who plays skillfully on the strings of their emotions and stirs the imaginations of their hearts. Every church board or local search committee is looking for a pastor who can preach, one the people will turn out to hear. These kinds of preachers are pampered, paid, promoted, and proclaimed, because many congregations believe a gifted speaker in the pulpit is to be desired above rubies and can compensate for the need for grass roots volunteers.

There is nothing wrong in seeking a gifted pastor who can draw people by his speaking ability and by the magnetism of his personality. We would all rather hear a sermon that communicates than one that doesn't. However, there is something wrong with depending on a brilliant preacher to fill the pews.

Passive, uninvolved listening is not what Jesus had in mind when He filled the place with His presence on Pentecost Sunday. He expected each person in His Church to be a minister, afire by His Spirit from within. What would happen if suddenly the roster of ministers in local congregations expanded to include scores and hundreds of laypersons who were spiritually active in the community seven days a week? I know of only two or three congregations who have caught this vision of lay ministry, and they are growing beyond any comparison with churches who are trying to grow through a pulpit-controlled ministry.

What if the proclamation of the gospel in a local congregation no longer depended on one special person, a former layperson who was educated for the ministry according to the standards set down by the hierarchy of the church, was then ordained and placed behind a pulpit as a magnet to draw the people into the church? What would happen if the proclamation of the gospel were suddenly a people explosion, a movement of lay volunteers? The kind of evangelism explosion Jesus must have had in mind happens when a gathering of His people, however small or large, becomes an excited army of pilgrims and proclaimers. A new explosion of Christian growth, in most congregations, will come with a new burst of Christian volunteering.

Years ago when our family moved to Boston, I took our sons to visit the famous Trinity Church, where Phillips Brooks was pastor from 1869 to 1891. Pastor Brooks's church made a dominant witness in the city of Boston when Trinity Church only seated 400 people, and there was no second service. In explaining this phenomenon of a disproportionate impact on the city of Boston for the size of his church, Phillips Brooks said, "I preach to 400 people every Sunday who repreach my sermon all week long." His sermon was repeated all over the city of Boston by a host of lay ministers.

I particularly wanted to show the boys the statue of Pastor Phillips Brooks looking out toward the city of Boston. Behind the pastor is a larger statue of Christ with Christ's hand resting on Phillips Brooks's shoulder. To me, the symbolism is unmistakable. The hand of Christ is on the shoulder of the pastor who reaches out to the community with a church full of lay volunteers who become His hands and feet all week while they preach again, and again, the message He has given them.

DEFEATED BY DISAPPOINTMENT

Some people have stopped volunteering because of a disappointing experience in their local church or in some other local church where they formerly served as a volunteer. They tried to be an extra voice in the choir or an additional pair of hands with a paintbrush but quit their assignment when their own personal expectations were not met, or when their work was criticized or rejected. No one is more difficult to motivate than someone who has been disappointed in his previous experience as a volunteer.

When Jesus encountered Cleopas and his companion on their way home from Jerusalem to Emmaus, their lament was, "We trusted that it had been he" (Luke 24:21). They went to Jerusalem looking for the Messiah but gave up in disappointment when they saw Him on the Cross.

They gave up because their expectations were not matched by their experience.

Dr. Luke's account of these two pilgrims en route home from Jerusalem is a classic account of what happens to disappointed volunteers. While traveling the road to Emmaus, they forgot their intentions to volunteer and returned home, having caved in to their own disappointment (Luke 24:13-24).

To begin with, Cleopas and his friend must have felt as if they had literally gone the extra mile. It was a 14-mile round trip to Jerusalem from Emmaus. This journey on foot was only made by people with a clear purpose. These two had put forth great effort to be in Jerusalem, where they could volunteer their service to Jesus, a man who was known for His miraculous healings, who loved the ordinary people, was known far and wide as a great teacher, and most of all, had gained the attention, if not the respect, of the rulers. There had been no other prospective Messiah who had so much to recommend Him.

But now Cleopas and his friend were on their way back home, footsore and depressed. Nothing creates physical and emotional fatigue more quickly than disappointment. But these men had plenty to say as "they talked together of all these things which had happened" (v. 14). Mutual disappointment creates a strong bond among people who are mutually hurt through the same disappointing experience.

They were disappointed because Jesus had not stood up to the leaders who had done Him in. "Our rulers delivered him to be condemned to death, and have crucified him" (v. 20). If He could have called 10,000 angels, why didn't He?

They were disappointed because their trust had been ill-placed. "But we trusted that it had been he which should have redeemed Israel" (v. 21). Cleopas and his friend are not the only volunteers who have gone home because they trusted the leader to deliver on unreal expectations.

These two on the Emmaus road turned homeward because their patience was too short and their waiting time too brief. "And beside all this, to day is the third day since these things were done."

They were disappointed because they had no vision. All they saw was an empty tomb, which they took as a sign of defeat and not a symbol of victory. "And when they found not his body . . . certain of them which were with us went to the sepulchre, and found it even so as the women had said: but him they saw not" (vv. 23-24).

However, the way back to a new commitment by Cleopas and his friend is more challenging and instructing than the demise of their faith (Luke 24:25-35).

First, they got a new perspective. "And beginning at Moses and all the prophets, he expounded unto them in all the scriptures the things concerning himself" (v. 27). These men began to see where the Cross fit into the total scheme of things.

Second, they got a new vision. "And it came to pass, as he sat at meat with them, he took bread, and blessed it, and brake, and gave to them. And their eyes were opened, and they knew him; and he vanished out of their sight" (vv. 30-31). It is amazing what happens when spiritual blindness is healed by the power of Christ.

And, with their new perspective and their new vision, they suddenly had new energy and enthusiasm. "And they rose up the same hour, and returned to Jerusalem" (v. 33). And suddenly, they now had the motivation for another seven-mile walk.

Recruiting disappointed former volunteers takes time and patience. But they are worth the effort, even if the fruit of their service has lain dormant for years because of disappointment.

NO TIME TO VOLUNTEER

There is a third good reason why church members are not volunteering. It is the myth that says church people these days are too busy to volunteer. And far too many of us have believed this myth. "It's not like it used to be in the old days." "People live too far from the church." "Commuting takes all the extra time people might use in Christian service."

But facts do not back up this myth. Dr. John Robinson, of the University of Maryland, directed a significant research project that refutes the myth of not enough time to volunteer. As reported in The *Journal of American Demographics* (July 1989), his study included 5,000 people who kept diaries on the use of their time. After accounting for all their hours (1) working, (2) commuting, (3) sleeping, and (4) caring for household duties, the average person has about 40 hours of discretionary time each week that they can choose to use for (1) additional paid or unpaid work, or (2) leisure time for such things as watching television, sports, hobbies, or whatever. All of us who live under the myth of being too busy to volunteer need to stop and do an accounting of our time.

According to Dr. Robinson's study, men have 40 hours of personal time, up 2 hours in the last decade. Women have 39 hours of personal time, up 5 hours since 1965. People in the 41-64 age bracket have the biggest increase in personal time, up 8 hours since 1965. The only group who lost personal time, not surprisingly, are the parents of preschoolers who lost several hours, down to 31 for men and 34 for women, in the last decade.

According to Dr. Robinson, many wrongly think leisure or personal time is dwindling because of the media's preoccupation with the workaholic yuppies. The fact is, most of us have time to volunteer if we are motivated to do so.

DEAF EARS AND BLIND EYES

Some church members never volunteer, or have quit volunteering, because they have not heard the call or seen the vision. They may take on certain assignments in the church from time to time, but they have never heard the call to volunteerism as a way of life.

By coincidence, President George Bush made a national call for volunteers during the week Nazarenes were gathered for the General Assembly in Indianapolis in 1989. I can only wish we all could have heard the call for service to our country and to our churches. In a speech delivered to civic leaders in New York, Mr. Bush said, "I ask all Americans to make service central to your life and work." He said volunteerism was not a program, or a bureaucracy, but a movement. "To every corporation I say: Begin a literacy program. To every member of a body of higher learning: Start a Big Brother or a Big Sister program. Of every church and synagogue I ask: Become an around-the-clock community center." In Washington, Sen. Edward Kennedy responded for himself and the opposition party by praising the leadership of Bush on the issue. He said, "The idea of service to others is a reflection of America at its best."

The challenge by President Bush could be readily translated into church language when he said, "There is no problem in America that is not being solved somewhere." Translated, this means, there is no challenge faced by any local church that is not being solved somewhere, by dedicated volunteers. (Source: *Indianapolis Star,* June 23, 1989.)

I have known of churches who have seen the vision and heard Christ's word, "Even so send I you" (John 20:21). No one knows how effective a local church could become if the entire congregation could be mobilized toward a common goal. The potential results are beyond our imagination.

RETURN ON INVESTMENT

When President Kennedy challenged Americans to join the Peace Corps for two years of voluntary service, people responded by the hundreds of thousands. The public was aghast at the overflowing response to a call for volunteers to serve in Third World circumstances, in subsistence living conditions, amid marginal conditions. Commentators, editorial writers, columnists, and talk show hosts filled the media with many versions of answers to the question: Why do people volunteer?

A variety of studies all led to the idea of return on investment. Simply stated: I am willing to volunteer my time, energy, and skills; but in return I expect something that may be a spiritual, psychological, social, or material return. People who volunteer expect a return on their investment. If the return is not adequate, they quit.

People joined the Peace Corps for two reasons. (1) They wanted to help the less fortunate. And, (2) in return they expected to receive a rewarding experience. For the most part, these volunteers were urged on by a humanitarian and pioneering spirit. Volunteering for these people was a challenge and a chance; a challenge to serve others and a personal risk in terms of returns.

As one volunteer put it, "I have chosen the possibility of a challenging and rewarding experience to serve . . . and such a choice always involves risk . . . at this point I feel I can afford the risk" (Joseph Coleman, "A Discovery of Commitment").

Most notable in Dr. Coleman's study was the contrast in giving and receiving. More than 93% of the applicants who filled out 12 pages of forms reported "a desire to give" as basic in their reasons for applying to the Peace Corps. Only 63% wrote about what they expected to gain from the experience. And only 6% wrote a "getting" statement on what they hoped to receive from the Peace Corps experience without writing about what they expected to give. However, 33% wrote a giving statement without writing about what they expected to receive. Peace Corps volunteers were weighted on the side of investment, not return.

These Peace Corps people were not bland volunteers who faded into the landscape of public service. They were well-educated people, highly motivated by humanitarian concerns, but they expected an experience of personal growth and increased satisfactions in return. This is what is called return on investment.

When Lyndon Johnson addressed a gathering of Peace Corps volunteers, he said: "I flatly refuse to ask you, why did you join the Peace Corps? I understand you expect that question." Then the president went on to remind the volunteers of the exchange between Thoreau, who was in the Concord jail for protesting injustice, and his friend Emerson, who came to visit. "My dear Thoreau," Emerson said, "why are you here?" And Thoreau replied, "My dear Emerson, why are you not here?" There is something about volunteering that is right. Volunteering needs no defense.

A PRIVATE WORD TO PASTORS

Everybody needs a support system. No pastor is an island. None of us can make it alone. Even the activities like swimming and weight lifting, which can be done alone, are done best in company with others. Jesus did not work alone. He was supported by volunteers, usually the Twelve, sometimes only the Three—Peter, James, and John—and once in Galilee by 70 whom He sent out in pairs. Mary, Martha, and Lazarus made their home a refuge for Him on His visits to Jerusalem.

Paul is almost always mentioned with others who volunteered to work with him. There were men like Barnabas, Silas, Luke, and Mark. In Philippi his work was greatly assisted by a businesswoman, Lydia. Women like Lois and Eunice, the grandmother and mother of Timothy, welcomed him into the hospitality of their homes.

Don't try to make it alone. Enlist the help of the best people you know, and train them adequately in the ways of Christian service. Willing volunteers who see their work as important will extend the time and energy of the church, and yourself. Programs may attract people to your church but it is people who keep people coming. People may be attracted to the church by colorful and helpful worship services. But they will be retained in the church when they become involved with a small group of serving church members whom they enjoy. A Christian becomes a productive church member when he becomes an enthusiastic volunteer. People do not bond to an entire congregation. They bond to a small group within the congregation with whom they can fellowship and work.

5

The Problem of
Human Frailty

When Jesus recruited the 12 volunteers who became His apostles, He challenged them to a higher calling and more fulfilling work than their regular jobs could offer.

Matthew was called from a customs gate on the territorial border of Galilee. Jews like Matthew, who sold out to the Romans as tax collectors and customs agents, were despised by their countrymen. Their lives were filled with authority but very little else. Every transaction at the customs gate was a crisis. Every day was a succession of crises with loud exchanges designed to raise the blood pressure, stretch the nerves, and increase the level of stress. Their job was to fix a value on all goods passing through the gate and then tax it accordingly. Agents became the object of wrath from travelers who were sure they were being gouged. Matthew's personal satisfactions on the job must have been meager.

Therefore, Matthew, like many other people with unfulfilling jobs, was susceptible to volunteering when Jesus stopped at his customs gate. While paying His own tax, Jesus must have observed the frustration in Matthew's body language. As He read unhappiness in the face of the Jewish agent, Jesus entered into a conversation that finally led to the cryptic invitation, "Follow Me." According to the New Testament account, it seems Matthew just walked away from his dehumanizing job and volunteered on the spot to follow a higher calling.

Peter, James, and John were in a different kind of work from Matthew. Nonetheless their careers in the fishing business had apparently failed to satisfy their inmost needs. They yelled a lot. James and John were called the Sons of Thunder. They were frustrated. Sometimes they toiled all night and caught no fish. Sometimes they were bored. Daytimes were spent in uninspiring jobs like repairing nets and maintaining boats. And there was the predictable haggling over the price of fish and the sometimes impossible demands for on-time deliveries. They had their own business, but as frustrated persons their aspirations were drowning in a sea of unfulfilled needs.

Andrew's excitement at the prospects of a higher calling sent him to bring his older brother, Peter, to meet Jesus. In this case one volunteer brought in another, which is still the pattern for church growth 2,000 years later.

Eventually the breakdown in loyalty among Jesus' volunteers come over problems in personal expectations. Judas turned against Jesus and sold Him out because he saw no self-serving future in following Him. At the beginning he must have volunteered because of the higher call he saw in following Jesus. But in the end his expectations and his desire for money got in the way.

Peter, in many ways, was a failure. He fell asleep in Gethsemane on the night Jesus needed him most. He followed afar off when Jesus was en route to the place of His final agony. In the courtyard of Caiaphas the high priest, Peter cursed and then denounced his loyalty to Jesus because of the pressure from hostile company.

James and John sent their mother to ask favors of Jesus. They wanted to be the number two and number three men in the administrative structure around Him. They had a wrong idea of what Jesus was about. They thought He would run the Romans into the Mediterranean and restore political power to the Jews. They missed the whole idea of a spiritual kingdom, God's kingdom in the hearts of men and women.

The disciples originally volunteered because Christ called them to a higher life. But Judas abandoned Jesus, and the rest of them entertained thoughts of quitting when their expectations were not met. This contradiction of volunteering for Christian service because of the higher calling it affords and then quitting or turning on leadership because of unfulfilled expectations is still alive. How many church members have volunteered to teach children because of the idealism this kind of volunteering supposes? And how many have dropped out of service because of breakdowns in communications, personality conflicts with colleagues, incompatible facilities, lack of recognition, or disillusion over results?

People volunteer for a higher reason, to fill a void in their life, and they quit for mundane reasons such as money problems or rank in the organization. These contradictory motivations among the disciples is a pattern that is still alive in the local church.

THE HUMAN FACTOR

Following Jesus may give a person new direction, but it does not change basic personality structure. Let's look at some examples: After following Jesus for nearly three years, Thomas still suffered from negativism that expressed itself in uncontrollable doubt. On the Sunday night of Jesus' resurrection, depression kept Thomas from the gathering of the disciples where Jesus personally appeared. Thomas later refused to believe Jesus was alive even when his best friends reported the fact. That's strong-minded negativism.

Peter was loud, intimidating, and unpredictable. He proclaimed his loyalty to Jesus publicly, but he let Him down privately. Peter could walk on water and fall under its waves in successive moments.

Andrew's loving personality served him well. He played second fiddle to his older brother, Peter, and never seemed to mind. He fit in wherever he was needed. He introduced the Greeks to Jesus but pulled back without demanding special recognition.

In summary: Volunteering to follow Jesus changes the direction of our lives, but it does not change anyone's basic personality structure.

THE DIFFERENCE AFTER PENTECOST

No one can study the motivations of the disciples and ignore what happened to them at Pentecost. If following Jesus gave direction to their lives, being cleansed and filled with His presence provided them power for His service.

Peter, who wilted under the heat of peer pressure in the high priest's courtyard, became Peter, the first public proclaimer of the gospel. In Jerusalem, where Jesus had been crucified and where His enemies were still roaming in the streets, Peter made himself vulnerable by "standing up" to preach, "lift[ing] up his voice" to be clearly heard (Acts 2:14), and proclaiming Christ as the Messiah with power and conviction that resulted in the conversion of several thousand people (vv. 14-41).

After Peter's sermon on Pentecost Sunday, he was a marked man. But it did not seem to matter. When he was finally arrested in Rome, the world headquarters for Christian hostility, Peter did not flinch but, by tradition, asked to be crucified head down, unworthy to be crucified as his Lord.

Thomas, who was plagued by doubt and depression, left Jerusalem after Pentecost and preached in the nations to the south and east, where he is credited with the establishment of the church in India. As a volunteer he poured out his life in ministry that never gained him the recognition he deserved.

James and John, who sought recognition and power through their mother, never strove for either in their service to Christ after Pentecost. James became the first apostle to be martyred, being slain by Herod's sword. John outlived all the other disciples as a teacher in Ephesus. He became the man behind the Gospel that bears his name, and he served as the guardian of Mary the mother of Jesus.

HUMAN FRAILTY

The presence of Christ's Spirit, who cleansed and filled the disciples on Pentecost, was the Source of power for their lives of voluntary service. But the fullness of the Spirit did not save the disciples or the first generation of Christians from the frailties of being human.

For instance, 10 years after Pentecost, Peter still did battle with his prejudice against Romans, especially the soldiers in the army of occupation. Cornelius, one of the Roman officers stationed in Caesarea, became interested in Christ and His gospel. Like any man in high authority, Cornelius sent for the top man, Peter, who was the best-known Christian leader in Israel. At the time Cornelius needed help, Peter was staying in the home of a friend, Simon, who operated a tanning business in a seacoast town some distance south of Caesarea.

Peter's intuitive response to the call from the Gentile, Cornelius, was negative. Not until God had taught Peter a special antiprejudice lesson could Peter leave with the messengers of Cornelius, to offer the gospel to (1) this Gentile, (2) a Roman, and (3) an officer in the army that occupied Peter's country. God's lesson that Peter had to learn was plain but difficult. "Ye know how that it is an unlawful thing for a man that is a Jew to keep company, or come unto one of another nation; but God hath shewed me that I should not call any man common or unclean" (Acts 10:28).

Prejudice was not the only problem in the hearts of these early Christians. John Mark was overcome by homesicknesses in Perga during his trip with Paul and Barnabas to what is now called Turkey. Even though he had volunteered for the journey, John Mark suddenly gave in to his feelings and left Paul and his Uncle Barnabas for the comforts of his mother's big house in Jerusalem (Acts 13:13).

Sometime later, after the General Assembly in Jerusalem when difficult issues on grace and law were hotly debated (Acts 15), Paul was assigned the task of informing the churches in Asia Minor (Turkey) about the understanding the delegates had reached in Jerusalem.

When Paul asked Barnabas to be his partner as he had on their previous journey to Cyprus and Galatia, Barnabas insisted on giving John Mark a second chance by inviting the young man to join them. Paul was adamantly opposed. Since Mark had turned homesick and left them on their previous journey, why wouldn't he do it again? And furthermore Mark didn't deserve a second chance. Paul and Barnabas exchanged strong words. I don't know who overspoke, but Paul and Barnabas separated company. Barnabas and his nephew, John Mark, sailed off to Cyprus and into oblivion in the New Testament narrative. Paul got a new partner named Silas, and together they left on foot for Antioch.

Apparently, Pentecost did not make the early Christians agree, even on major issues. Everything was not smooth. The two giant leaders, Peter and Paul, had a confrontation. A terse account of their confrontation in Paul's own words stirs the imagination on what the situation was like when these two giants of faith crossed swords: "But when Peter was come to Antioch, I withstood him to the face, because he was to be blamed" (Gal. 2:11).

The Early Church also faced many other problems caused by human frailty. (1) Ananias and Sapphira volunteered to give all the proceeds from the sale of their house to the church. Then for their own reasons they held back part of the price (Acts 5). (2) In the original congregation in Jerusalem, there was so much complaining among the widows over the distribution of compassionate ministries money among the newcomers from the broader Greek world, the Jerusalem church had to stop its work to elect a board to look after the matter so that the apostles could give their time more fully to prayer and ministry of the Word (Acts 6). And thus the first church board was born.

Summary: There is no need to push the evidence for this truth further. After the baptism with the Holy Spirit, volunteers still evidenced the problems that come with being human. The experience of entire sanctification cleanses and empowers the will for Christian service. But there is no promise that voluntary service of church members will run smoothly just because the volunteers are Christians with good intentions.

There are two kinds of motivations for Christians who volunteer their services in the church. (1) They volunteer because of their love for Christ and the call to serve Him through the church. (2) And they also volunteer because of the human needs their church programs are designed to meet. Although some church members volunteer for human reasons such as recognition and friendship, the motive that most often prevails is love of Christ and commitment to the local church. The reason good Christians quit their volunteer jobs in the church may be a breakdown in their faith, but it is more likely to be a deterioration in the human satisfactions they are receiving from their assignments. After all, they are human.

THE SPECTACULAR POWER
OF COMMITMENT

In spite of human frailty, church members continue to volunteer. When there were ample reasons for the Early Church to be at each other's throats, they continued to volunteer their service with telling effectiveness.

The question is: Why?

Why didn't they burn up their energies on each other in hostile church battles instead of pouring themselves into sacrificial Christian service? Why didn't they short-circuit their work by legislating the detailed and meticulous Jewish law on such things as Sabbath observance, the keeping of special ceremonial days on the religious calendar, and other rules that consumed the minds of the Jews?

The early Christians could have destroyed the Church over personal differences like those that separated Paul and Barnabas, or caused the widows in the Jerusalem church to keep up their murmuring against the distribution system and against each other. But none of these manifestations of human frailty prevailed. The members of the Early Church overcame their human relations problems, their theological concerns, and their church structure problems, while they continued to pour out their lives in voluntary service for Christ and His Church.

There are several reasons why these first-century church members overcame their differences in favor of voluntary Christian service. But the first reason was commitment that never wavered. With the early Christians faith and service were opposite sides of the same coin. If you loved Christ, you served Him. They disagreed on many things, but no difference of opinion canceled their commitment to serve Christ and the church.

Their commitment to Christ and the church was like the commitment of a mature married couple whose disagreements may be intense but never a reason or occasion to threaten their commitment to each other and to their marriage. Across the years, every local church has good times and bad times, peak times and valley times. However, the volunteers who never question their commitment in spite of changing conditions in the local church are the people with internal control beyond the reach of external heat or cold.

THE FOCUS ON PEOPLE

Another factor that saved the Early Church volunteers from the ravages that would have led them to self-destruct over problems created by the human condition was their concern for people and not for construction projects. The focus of volunteer service in the Early Church was on people. For the first 300 years of the church's history, no sanctuaries were constructed. There were no national or regional administrative headquarters. There were no designated hierarchies with levels of status and power. The church was people serving people.

All of the pomp and ceremony, construction of great church edifices, and hierarchy of structure came first with the conversion of the Emperor Constantine in A.D. 325. With the eventual decline of the Roman Empire the church inherited its monolithic structure of power and authority. And from then until now, the biggest battle the church fights is to keep itself people centered.

When Christians in the Early Church volunteered to serve, they didn't define their voluntary service to Christ in terms of free labor on construction projects. They did not spend long evenings in unsettling church board meetings. When early Christians volunteered to serve, they were volunteering to serve people. They had no high-tech offices, no elaborate worship service productions that required great amounts of advance planning. They burned up their spiritual energies serving people who needed to be saved and established in grace.

There is no way Christian congregations today are going back to the house-church idea. These are different times. People have different expectations. But the church that reaps the most benefit from its volunteers is the one with the strongest focus on people. As Christ volunteered himself to redeem the lives of people, Christians in the 1st century and in the 21st century volunteer their lives in His service. We are the only hands and feet Christ has on earth.

A closing word: It is a shame, and just short of a tragedy, for volunteer programs in modern churches to be disrespected and in some instances destroyed by theological controversy, quarrels over standards, and piques over bruises to the ego. The devil laughs and the world ridicules the congregation that allows its internal differences to destroy its Christian usefulness. But churches who are sloshing along with no growth statistics and rationalizing their empty altars need to understand how people in the Early Church handled their differences while they continued to serve Christ.

III

A Perspective on Motivation Among Volunteers

6

Cultivating the Soil

I might have accepted the 80/20 principle as normal until I read about a church where everyone volunteered. They outstripped the ratio of one volunteer in each three religious people as set down in the good Samaritan story. People in this church could have defended their reluctance to volunteer, and all outside observers would have supported them. However, these church members stepped forward to volunteer when it meant laying their lives on the line.

THE ROMANIAN CHURCH

Since the days of the Romans, who fed their Christians to the lions, no country has surpassed Communist Romania in oppressing evangelical religion. The clampdown started in 1947, when Communist rule was imposed following the Yalta agreements. For the next 42 years, Christmas was obliterated from the official calendar, and Christians who loved their Bibles had to go underground or endure the unrelenting harassment of the government.

For 24 years, under the tyrannical rule of Nicolae Ceauşescu (chow-SHESS-coo), the Baptist church, which was the most visible denomination in Romania, suffered the most. Police cars were regularly parked outside their doors. Entering worshipers were photographed and identified. The phones of volunteer lay leaders were tapped. Their work was hampered by laws against the possession of Bibles and evangelical Christian books. Every sermon was audited by the secret police. And pastors were even prohibited from preaching or referring to the Book of Revelation because Ceauşescu did not like its focus on the second coming of Christ and promises of hope for deliverance of oppressed people.

When the Baptist people built a new church in Comăneşti, 135 miles north of Bucharest, the government tore it down after completion, accusing the congregational leaders of "stealing construction materials and other socialist property." Four of their leaders were sent to prison. However, within two weeks after the fall of Ceauşescu, on December 22, 1989, the political prisoners were released, and people walked the main boulevards of the cities, waving the long-denied Christmas symbols. And on December 31, in Oradea, a northwestern city of Romania, 10,000 worshipers packed a sports arena for a Christian rally with the permission of the new government. What a miracle!

It was no less a miracle, however, that Baptist membership under two decades of Ceauşescu's oppression went from 60,000 to 300,000, an increase of 500%. The haunting question is: Why?

The simplistic answer is: Persecution.

To some degree persecution may be the answer. But harassment, brutality, and jail sentences are by no means all of the explanation. Part of the answer may be found in an observation by Slobadan Lekie, who wrote the story for the Associated Press. He said, "The Romanian Orthodox church was treated more leniently because it generally limited itself to such traditional ceremonies as mass, marriages, and funerals." Apparently, a traditional church that does little more than hold customary services and perform its functions in marriage and death is no threat to an anti-Christian regime. Churches with ceremonial religion do not need to be restricted by alien governments. They have already restricted themselves by the nature of their faith. Their prison bars have been forged on their own anvils.

Pastor Ilie Tundrea of the Bethany Baptist Church gives a hint at what made the growth difference among Baptist churches. He said the woeful lack of Bibles and good Christian books was partially made up by European Christians who smuggled in the much-needed religious materials in secret compartments in their vans. Baptist pastors were arrested if caught distributing these books and Bibles, but apparently this was a risk they were willing to take. Why? Because Baptist volunteers were using these books and Bibles to disciple new Christians.

Ceauşescu stopped the free use of the pulpit, but he did not understand the power of the volunteer who was willing to give his time and energy in the low-profile work of discipling. Ceauşescu could stop the public reading of the Book of Revelation, but he did not think about the private volunteers who knew how to use a personal relationship in winning Christian converts and establishing them in the faith. What the pulpit could not do, the local church volunteer could.

This overwhelming growth of Romanian Baptists through a program of voluntary discipling should not be a surprise. This was the method of the Early Church in Jerusalem and Samaria. There are reports of great gatherings in Jerusalem with thousands of converts. But there is no indication in the New Testament of an ancient counterpart of the great preacher, superchurch, televangelist syndrome. Charisma was not a personality characteristic but a relationship in the Holy Spirit. The continuing work of the Church in building faith among early Christians was carried out in homes where willing volunteers discipled new members. The Christians in the cities and in the countryside broke bread from house to house, both the bread of heaven and the bread of human fellowship, sometimes served from the kitchen and sometimes from the Word of God. The

Church in the 1st century and in the 21st does not thrive on reluctant volunteers but by committed volunteers.

THE IDEAL CONGREGATION

Many a pastor has fantasized about the utopian church where everyone is a volunteer (1) who wins converts to Christ, (2) then volunteers the time to disciple the new Christian into a stable, faithful, church member, and (3) who in turn wins new converts and disciples them into soul-winning followers of Christ, as the cycle of church growth expands. With the possible exception of the evangelical church in Romania under Ceaușescu, several things keep this ideal from happening:

Church Members but Not Disciples

Unfortunately, church membership roles include great numbers of people who have never been discipled themselves. Like the Christians in Corinth, many modern church members are faithful to a favorite pastor who did things the way they liked them done. Or, they are drawn to a church by the music and sit in judgment on any changes in format or platform procedures that go against their churchly nerves. There are church members in abundance whose loyalty is bonded to a specific congregation by the unreliable glue of a magnetic personality in the pulpit, a comforting emotional warmth in the service, and an informal theology that never gets in the way of how they want to live. These types of church people easily fade in and out of congregations with a touch-and-go level of voluntary service that falls several levels below a full Christian commitment. They are church members, but not disciples.

The Decency of a Church Connection

There are second- and third-generation church members in our congregations who have more interest in the decency of a church connection than a devotion to living its faith. The Puritans in Boston developed a Halfway Covenant for their second- and third-generation families who wanted a respectable connection with the church for baby dedications, funerals, and the like but did not want to pay the price of Christian involvement. Today, it is simply membership without responsibility.

Variety and Rigidity

In some churches, voluntary service is rigidly confined to one category of volunteering, such as Sunday School visitation. In this rigid setting, Monday night visitation becomes the litmus test of voluntary Christian service. These kinds of pastors have either ignored or forgotten the great variety among people. Everyone is different. There is variety in spiritual gifts. Not all the plants in God's garden bloom at the same time or flower in the same way. Everyone can be a volunteer, but not everyone can be a cold-turkey door-to-door church visitor or even a telemarketing volunteer. Pastors who want to motivate more volunteers in their local churches need to be flexible and let people develop the gift God gave them, not the gift the pastor wishes God had given them.

Every church includes several types of personalities who, by the fact of being human, respond to the challenge of volunteering within the limits of their own personality structure. Not everyone is a salesman, nor is everyone an accountant. Some church members who may be effective volunteers in one area of service would be predictable failures in others. The kitchen and the classroom call for different definitions of service. The cook and the teacher may work under the same administration of the Holy Spirit, but their jobs call for different gifts.

I am sure there were Baptists in Romania under Ceauşescu who did not do hands-on discipling. Some located safe homes. Others skillfully governed the supply of Bibles or staked out house meetings to warn the volunteers when police were in the area. And there must have been some who did most of their volunteering in the form of earning and donating the money that was in short supply.

There is no one single model of Christian volunteer service. There is variety among the Christians planted and blooming in God's garden. This variety is beautiful. It's a sight to stir the soul. If everyone had the same gift, the church would lose the inspiration of a rainbow.

God is not looking for look-alikes. It's not only the matter of differing gifts, which Paul explains in his letters to the Romans and the Ephesians, but also because of personality differences that some Christians are more likely to volunteer in one way and others in another. Beware of the pastor who is intent on making all volunteers serve in like manner. At best, the congregation will become lopsided.

A NEED FOR A SOIL TEST

The disparity between the potential and the actual number of practicing volunteers in a local church is a contradiction in the meaning of Christian. Someone explained this contradiction as the difference between the sunbathers on the beach and the swimmers in the water, or the athletes who talk a good game and those who play to win. Couch potatoes in church are as much of an anachronism as choir members who don't sing. There is a dramatic gap between the number of church members actually available for volunteering and the total number of people who could be volunteers if they were only motivated.

There is also a perceptible difference between the small amount of service by some church members and the extraordinary dedication in hours of work by others. On a scale of 1 to 10 (10 being the highest level of service), there are too many church members at both ends of the continuum and not enough in the middle. Jesus explained these differences in productivity by the variety of soils where seeds are sown.

Walking out on the dock at Capernaum where the fishing boats were tied, Jesus asked His friends to row Him out a few yards from the shore. Here He could be separated a discreet distance from the people while the still water, which is an excellent sounding board, amplified His voice to the host of people sitting on the shore.

Jesus did not tickle the ears of the crowd by ranting against the abuses of the Roman army of occupation. He did not whip the people into a frenzy by promising them health and prosperity, or make them feel guilty because they were sick or unemployed. Like Gideon, He sounded the trumpet that signaled the separation of those who could be counted on from those who could not. One-quarter of the crowd who volunteered to follow Him could be counted on to produce a harvest from 30-fold to 100-fold. However, the remainder of the crowd who listened would simply be (1) too hard, (2) too shallow, (3) or too busy to volunteer.

Jesus put this truth into a parable that every Galilean could understand fully. Some suggest He may have told His story while they watched a farmer sowing his seed in a nearby field. Whatever the mental picture, the people got the message about the seed and the four kinds of soil. (1) Some soil was hard, and the seed never took root. (2) Some soil was shallow, and the seed took root and sprang up quickly but soon died under the burning sun on shallow soil. (3) Still other seeds fell on thorny soil, where they could not be cultivated. (4) Finally, there was the good soil, which produced a bountiful harvest.

Some who had been following the ministry of Jesus for the loaves and fishes closed Him out of their hearts. They had volunteered only for what they could get out of it. When the prospects of the job benefits were reduced, they quit. Others who heard Him call for volunteers to "follow me" made quick, superficial responses that soon withered in the sun. They couldn't take the heat required to stand up for Jesus when the pressure was on. A third category who listened to Jesus really believed in Him, but their good intentions were soon choked out by the complications of responsibility to family and work. They were too busy. They were too involved in their own purposes to have time to serve Him. This contingent was never able to get their priorities straight. Everything they did competed for time and energy with everything else they did. They never figured out the difference between the urgent and the important. Since voluntary service to Jesus competed with everything else in their agenda, it was destined, by the nature of life, to come off second. But for one group, the call of Jesus for commitment became a lifelong motive. Their lives of Christian service brought forth 30-fold, 60-fold, and 100-fold in a harvest blessing.

Just how many times over is the life of a fruitful Sunday School teacher, youth worker, or family counselor multiplied through his voluntary service to Christ? The shoe cobbler, William Carey, multiplied his life 1,000 times over in the founding of the modern missionary movement. An unordained shoe salesman, Dwight L. Moody, geometrically expanded his life 1,000 times over in Chicago through the building of the world's largest Sunday School and a great church that specialized in reaching people who thought nobody loved them. In time, this evangelism stirred the spiritual heart of England and America as Moody spread the seed of the gospel. His short sermons were directed at the heart and met their mark among the rich and famous as well as urchins. Abraham Lincoln stopped off in Chicago to visit Moody's Sunday School en route to Washington as the president-elect of the United States.

Others in her Catholic order were more gifted than Mother Teresa, but she was more willing. She touched the untouchables. She loved the unlovely. She poured out her life on people who had no earthly way to repay her. With Mother Teresa, love was a way of life.

Billy Graham volunteered his life to Christ as a soul winner, not an intellectual or even a gifted preacher. And God multiplied the fruit of his ministry beyond count. Almost every great arena in the world has been filled with record-breaking crowds who came to hear him sow the seed for a new life in Christ.

There were other potential Dwight Moodys, Mother Teresas, and Billy Grahams. There may have been potential volunteers who were more talented, better educated, and more attractive than these great Christian leaders, but none more willing to serve.

LOVE AND GUILT

How much of our voluntary service is done out of guilt and how much is done out of love? The answer to this question of love and guilt in voluntary service is not simple. If we recognize the difference between (1) a theological state of guilt that is wiped clean through the blood of Christ, and (2) the psychological feelings of guilt we impose on ourselves anytime we fall short of our own standards of performance, then we understand why (3) every Christian copes with the stress generated by the opposing feelings of love and guilt.

According to Paul in his letter to the Romans, "There is therefore now no condemnation to them which are in Christ Jesus" (8:1). Paul's word is both comfort and confusion to many people. We find comfort in the fact that our sins are forgiven and we no longer stand condemned before God. But we are self-condemned for our many human failures.

The psychological goblins of "ought" and "should" tyrannize the minds and hearts of many good people. Many loyal church members live with a high level of anxiety because of their feelings of unworthiness, inferiority, and failure. They accept their roller coaster of mental and spiritual health as normal. We "should" be better parents than we are. We "ought" to get more done than we do. We "should" have been more Christian toward the person who criticized us—and on and on!

These psychological, self-imposed guilt feelings become the only soil many Christians have for cultivating their motivations for voluntary Christian service. They volunteer because volunteering helps get rid of the feelings of guilt that flood them if they don't. Unfortunately guilt motivation lacks durability. Christian service motivated by guilt is only useful in the short term. Guilt motivation dwindles to nothing after a reasonable level of volunteering is achieved. Among the guilty, motivation to volunteer begins to decrease as voluntary service increases. The person who feels guilty for not singing in the choir may volunteer to get rid of their guilt. But when the guilt is gone, they no longer feel the same motivation to sing in the choir.

Objective guilt is guilt over lying or stealing or any other personal action, or intended action, against the laws of God. We stand condemned by God's Word for the sins we have committed. This is deserved guilt, which calls for the remedy of repentance and godly forgiveness. We have all faced this state of guilt, and most of us have found freedom from this kind of condemnation through faith in the sacrifice of Christ for our sins.

But many of us have never found freedom from the condemnation we place upon ourselves because we "should" have done something we didn't do, such as spend more time with our children. Or we heap guilt on ourselves because we "ought" to be someone we really are not. Oftentimes we compare ourselves unfavorably to someone else—a homemaker, wage earner, or student. Even when we are successful, we may feel guilty because we are not more successful than we are, or because success was slow in coming.

Unfortunately, the mind does not know the difference between the feelings that are rooted in objective guilt that come from breaking the Ten Commandments, and the psychological feelings of guilt that come from breaking our own self-imposed standards. The feelings are the same. And either kind of guilt frustrates the motivating love of God in our lives.

A person who has a strong feeling of love and a low residue of guilt will respond in a different way to the pastor's challenge for volunteering than another church member who is dominated by incessant feelings of guilt and at the same time lives with a low level of love toward others. This is why some Christians volunteer out of love and others volunteer out of guilt.

The pastor who heaps guilt on his people as a means for motivating them to Christian service is not challenging them to offer a cup of cold water to a thirsty person out of love for Christ. Instead, he says, "Because there are so many people who need cold water, you should feel guilty if you don't get on with the business of giving away water when you have more for yourself than you can use." Or "You ought to do more for the missionary work in India because you have too much and they don't have enough." Many Christians will give cold water or send missionary money to India to get rid of the guilt that comes if they don't. Their giving is not a reliable indicator of their love.

THE FOURTH KIND OF LOVE

In the ancient world three words for love were commonly used in street conversation: (1) There was a word for erotic love. This was the love of a man for a maiden. This is the love of sexual attraction. (2) There was also a word for family love. This was the love people had for each other in the legal bonds of family. These bonds included husbands and wives, parents and children, grandchildren, brothers and sisters, plus a somewhat less effectual bond with in-laws, those who became part of the family by marriage. The love family members had for each other was special and highly prized. (3) Then there was a word for love in friendship. Most people have many associates, colleagues, and acquaintances, but only a few close personal friends. The love expressed to friends is different from either erotic love or family love. But love in a lasting friendship is a very important kind of love.

Each of these three loves—erotic, family, and friendship—is different, but each of them has one quality in common: Each of these loves is reciprocal. These three kinds of love depend on having someone to love in return. Erotic love calls for a sex partner. Family love depends on persons who want to sustain family relationships. And friendship requires reciprocity.

Jesus came into the world with a whole new meaning for love. His love, *agape*, is an unbeatable goodwill that is unconditional. (1) Christian love keeps on loving whether or not the person who receives it is deserving. Jesus prayed for the men who rejoiced at His crucifixion: "Father, forgive them; for they know not what they do" (Luke 23:34). (2) The love of Christ keeps on loving whether or not His love is returned. Christian love is not reciprocal. The love of Christ is likened to the "hound of heaven" that follows each of us relentlessly. This Christian love may be ignored, resisted, or rejected, but it cannot be obliterated.

Paul said it best: "Nay, in all these things we are more than conquerors through him that loved us. For I am persuaded, that neither death, nor life, nor angels, nor principalities, nor powers, nor things present, nor things to come, nor height, nor depth, nor any other creature, shall be able to separate us from the love of God, which is in Christ Jesus our Lord" (Rom. 8:37-39).

The greatest hindrance to the manifestation of this unconditional love in the lives of Christ's followers is guilt. This guilt may be objective or subjective, real or self-imposed, godly or human, but the consequences are the same. It leads to feelings of blame, denial, and unworthiness. As has been noted, the human mind doesn't know the difference between the feelings of guilt that come in breaking God's objective laws and the feelings of guilt that are self-imposed by falling short of our own standards. Guilt that comes from walking against God's law is therapeutic because it can lead to repentance and forgiveness. But guilt that comes from breaking your own self-imposed standards can lead to spiritual debilitation. All of us know people with enough physical energy to walk and run, but who are spiritually crippled because of their unresolved guilt.

Love and Guilt
in Motivating Volunteers

In a recent doctoral study on love and guilt, Les Parrott III surveyed more than 1,000 laymen who regularly attend one of five Churches of the Nazarene: First Churches in Portland and Salem, Oreg.; Chicago; Detroit; and Seymour, Ind. In his study of these laymen, he identified love and guilt in the four combinations that are represented in every congregation of potential volunteers.

In each congregation, there were significant groups of volunteers or potential volunteer laypersons who could be identified by their feelings of love and guilt. Each group was different from the others, sometimes in dramatic ways. And each of these groups represented a different kind of soil in which the seeds of volunteerism would take root and grow, or never grow at all.

LOW LOVE AND HIGH GUILT

Church members who are dominated by high levels of guilt but suffer a low level of love are not very good candidates for volunteer service. Pastors may plant good seed in the minds of these "high guilt and low love" people, but the seed is not likely to germinate and grow. These "low love and high guilt" people are already consumed with the business of trying to deal with the problems that stem from their guilt.

These Christians who are low on love and high on guilt may appear self-centered. They may appear punitive in their attitudes toward pastors and other authority figures. They survive by taking out their own feelings of guilt on others. One of the most popular tools for these kinds of people is projection. They like to see their problem as somebody else's fault. Pastors and other authority figures are often the objects of their wrath. These kinds of guilty people make their problem your problem.

Of the four dispositions in the congregation, these punitive people feel the most vulnerable and tend to be most defensive. Some pastors would rather they did not volunteer at all because their attitudes, behavior patterns, and episodes of anger only complicate matters for other volunteers. They are usually a part of the problem but seldom a part of the solution. These people are like the hard soil in Jesus' parable. The seeds of compassion never get a chance to germinate and grow within them, for their soil is hardened by guilt. The softening agent of love is scarce.

Punitive people tend to be cautious about relationships, separating themselves from others. They are not necessarily selfish, just private. They are afraid of being hurt in a relationship. As a result, they keep themselves uninvolved, isolated loners. Punitive, egocentric church members may function in a cooperative, pleasant manner on the surface but will not get involved in conversations of a personal nature. Questions about their lives are considered as intrusions on their privacy.

This protective privacy may appear in the "low love and high guilt" person as self-assurance, when this person is actually suffering deep anxiety and pain. This kind of person—"low love and high guilt"—has submerged undesirable emotions that he is afraid will come out in serious conversations. Therefore, he tends to have "great hellos" and "great good-byes" without much in between.

"Low love and high guilt" church members show little emotion about other people's problems and needs. They are not involved analytically with others, since they have no motivation to help sort out and understand the concerns of another person. They protect themselves by avoiding meaningful relationships altogether. If they volunteer at all, it is with little commitment. They evade issues and concerns in the church and protect their vulnerability by withdrawing from involvement. Don't expect much voluntary help from these kinds of members. Among all Nazarenes in the study, approximately 17% were punitive, "low love and high guilt" persons.

HIGH LOVE AND HIGH GUILT

The next personality we'll look at among church members is the "high love and high guilt" group. They place high value on Christian acts of love, but their loving is frustrated by equally strong feelings of guilt. Their responses to the needs of others are usually motivated by emotion. They welcome acts of self-sacrifice as expressions of their love. This feeling of sacrificial service is a kind of penance for their feelings of guilt. It is easy for these people to slip into self-righteous pride: "I must be a loving person because I have sacrificed so much to help others." These people are like the shallow soil in Jesus' parable where the seeds took root but were choked out by the suffocating cares of life.

Persons who experience feelings of "high love and high guilt" seem to go through cycles of guilt and love. Because they feel guilty, they do loving things; and because they do not express enough love, they feel guilty—and the cycle starts all over again. These people experience a cycle of pain and relief that comes from a fear of not doing enough to earn God's love and the love of their family and friends.

This is why they take great pride in good deeds and acts of self-sacrifice.

These kinds of people tend to be driven by their strong feelings of emotion, which lead them to deal with guilt by covering it over, pretending things are OK, and then surrendering to the negative emotional pressure with gales of self-rejection. These are good candidates to become chronic seekers at the altar or regular entries in the pastor's counseling calendar.

To say the least, the "high love and high guilt" church members are up-and-down volunteers. They do best after a new touch during the revival, a fresh surrender, or another emotional spiritual experience. The pastor or church leader who works with this kind of volunteer needs to understand the agony in their cycles of love and guilt, which dominate their spurts of volunteerism. The proportion of Nazarenes in this study who were characterized by "high love and high guilt" was approximately 34%.

LOW LOVE AND LOW GUILT

There is a third category of potential volunteer in the church whose personal makeup is a combination of "low love and low guilt." This kind of person is almost always a strong individualist. He can identify with the problems and needs of others in an intellectual and understanding way but does not easily demonstrate feelings of warmth and concern. He does not often cry in public, and not often in private. The "low love and low guilt" church member has developed a conscience that is not plagued with feelings of subjective guilt. His analytical mind has sorted out the difference between an objective state of guilt in God's sight and the feelings of subjective, self-imposed guilt that come from his own human failure.

The "low love and low guilt" volunteers do not consider their Christian service as a sacrifice. They volunteer because they have analyzed the need and believe it is worthy.

They volunteer without feelings of sacrifice or much expression of emotion. They volunteer because they feel it is right for them to volunteer.

Because these individuals have analyzed the situation and do not move on emotion, strings are likely to be attached to their commitment for service. They usually function with a controlling social style. They are uncomfortable with the people who see themselves as self-sacrificing. If you need to do something and love to do it, then where is the sacrifice? They reason that love that has become a burden is not longer love, it has turned into duty.

Strong individualists will volunteer but may try to manipulate and control the situation and the other volunteers who participate with them. It's their nature to lead, and this need to lead may cause them to dominate others who work with them. Their pattern of communication is direct. They will pressure, threaten, blame, and criticize in order to get things done. From a Transactional Analysis perspective, the strong individualist says, "I'm OK and you're OK if you do what I want."

Strong individualists—"low love and low guilt"—can be very valuable people in a congregation. They are often business people, educators, or other professionals who have a successful track record. They will volunteer when they have analyzed the situation and believe in what they are being asked to do. But they will volunteer on their own terms. The proportion of Nazarenes in this study who are characterized as "low love and low guilt" is approximately 23%.

HIGH LOVE AND LOW GUILT

Finally, there are people in every congregation who are "high love and low guilt" people. These are the loving people in the congregation who are not thrown off balance by great surges of emotion, and neither are they plagued with lingering feelings of guilt. They are free indeed. They actually live what Paul wrote: "There is therefore now no condemnation to them which are in Christ Jesus" (Rom. 8:1). These are the people in Christ's parable who rendered 30-fold, 60-fold, or 100-fold.

The strong individualist (low love and low guilt) is self-assertive. The emotional person (high love and high guilt) is self-sacrificing. The loner (low love and high guilt) is self-centered. But the truly loving person who is free from guilt (high love and low guilt) is self-transcending.

The "high love and low guilt" volunteers will rise above their own needs and concerns to place themselves fully in the place of another. They practice empathy on a daily basis. Their accepting attitudes make it possible for them to stand in someone else's place, feel as they feel, and think as they think. They are free from the frustrations of those who are plagued by the question, "I know you're OK, but I wonder if I am."

The loving person does not build relationships for personal advantage. To the loving person, relationships are important, in and of themselves. People are important, not because they can be used for private purposes, but because they are people.

While the strong individualist represses the vulnerable emotions such as tenderness, visible caring, open sympathy, and human warmth, the loving person expresses these emotions openly and easily.

The loving person admits to having needs and frailties without feeling guilty about them. The loving person finds fulfillment in the process of learning to love through personal growth, not in achieving a static condition of love that can be observed, approved, and applauded. This "high love and low guilt" person is even more remarkable for being than doing. Their presence in a group or on a board makes everyone feel better. Volunteering is a natural result of their genuine interest in people. They are people persons in the fullest sense of the word. They communicate by clarifying, explaining, and negotiating, not by demanding, blaming, and criticizing. They feel sincerely, "I'm OK. However, if you're not OK, that's OK with me." Then they demonstrate without saying it, "I'll love you anyway."

Every pastor and church lay leader longs for a church filled with people who have worked through the challenges and problems of an understanding love and the offsetting feelings of guilt. We can only wish our congregations were entirely constituted of people who are high in qualities of an understanding love and low in guilt. In this study of Nazarene laymen, approximately 26% were "high love and low guilt" people.

Now let's look at the effect these four personality types have on the complexion of a congregation. Few, if any, churches are dominated by punitive persons who are private and withdrawn. If so, the church would soon die because there would be no strong, committed group at the center of things whose volunteering is stable and dependable enough to make the church function. If there were a congregation like this, it would be a pastor-centered cult where people come strictly for their needs to be met without a concern for others. In this kind of church, service would end with the benediction.

I have seen churches dominated by a continuing need for more emotion. At the same time there is very little need for knowledge, information, or scriptural understanding, and a comprehensive biblical theology is even lower on their ladder of concerns. Motivation for volunteering in this kind of church is usually based on guilt. First, the pastor makes the people feel guilty, believing they will then volunteer to do the loving acts they "ought" and "should" do. This kind of church can achieve remarkable short-term goals in selected areas of need, as in sacrificial giving for needy people in faraway places. Some evangelists, missionary speakers, and special workers are strong motivators among these people who must feel guilty about a need rather than understand it.

Churches dominated by strong individualists have a tough time. These kinds of persons are often intimidating to a pastor who may be a "low love and high guilt" person himself. It is even worse if the pastor spiritualizes emotional response as the primary response to the Holy Spirit. A strong individualist who is analytical and nonemotional is almost always a threat to a "high love and high guilt" pastor who expects everyone to respond emotionally to the needs of the church. Some pastors make it difficult for these strong individualists to survive in the congregation, and as a result these laymen often find a more accommodating congregational environment in some other church. With enough pressure the successful businessman or professional person will feel uncomfortable and leave the congregation, thus lowering the level of leadership in the offended church. The pastor justifies the loss of the family on the basis of low spirituality as judged by the lack of emotional responses and the inability or unwillingness of the strong individualist to show unconditional enthusiasm for the pastor and his church programs. Questions from these strong individualists are intimidating to a punitive or emotional pastor and are usually interpreted as expressions of disloyalty.

The strong individualist usually finds a safe haven in a large church where a loving pastor gives him an adequate level of human understanding. In this kind of positive relationship between the pastor and the layperson, the strong individualist fits in and in his own way becomes a willing volunteer. But God help the smaller church that is struggling to absorb a strong individualist. Sergeants and privates have a hard time standing up to majors and colonels!

FURTHER CONCLUSIONS
ON LOVE AND GUILT

In this study on love and guilt in five Nazarene churches, several interesting and helpful conclusions were reached beyond the identification of the four personality types we have characterized.

Guilt diminishes a person's capacity to transcend self-interest and engage in loving behavior. This was seen most clearly among people who had a strong desire to be loving and at the same time were depressed with a high level of guilt. With them, volunteering is a roller coaster ride over the emotional hills and valleys of love and guilt in recurring cycles. They are up one day and down the next. They are fully involved in Christian service under the leadership of one pastor and withdrawn and noncooperative under the leadership of another.

Levels of guilt vary from person to person. Some people who value loving traits in themselves and others frustrate love in themselves by their feelings of self-imposed guilt. It is hard to be loving and guilty at the same time because the reactions to guilt are negative and critical, while the responses to love are outgoing and accepting.

Most pastors and most laymen are confused about the theological state of guilt from which God saves us through faith in Christ, and the feelings of psychological guilt we experience when an internalized standard is compromised. Because of this confusion on the difference between the biblical state of guilt and self-imposed guilt, many Nazarene pastors and laymen simply reported they did not know if guilt was a good motivation for Christian service or not.

Guilt does not keep us from holding love as a high ideal. We can appreciate loving behavior in others even when we are not loving ourselves. Guilt may inhibit our capacity to love but not our appreciation for love as a way of life. Although I feel guilty, I may still want to be a loving person. However, the stress this conflict produces has its own punishments.

People with high levels of guilt find it difficult to be empathic. They cannot easily put themselves in the other person's shoes in a loving, understanding way. They may be emotionally moved about another person's plight but have difficulty in accurately understanding their real needs. They can feel sorry for people who hurt but not understand them enough to be helpful. They may feel for but not with him. Like the Levite, they can give a good lecture on the perils of the road without being involved in helping the person who is already the victim of these perils. Their loving behavior may, on the surface, appear more helpful than it really is. For instance, a grieving person may need understanding more than sympathy. A helping hand may be needed along with a holding hand.

The "high love and high guilt" people are more motivated to make themselves look good than they are to meet the needs of the hurting person. By acting in a loving way, they temporarily rid themselves of their guilt feelings. That is why they think they are loving when they are really using love toward others to serve their own needs. Loving others as a means for removing guilt can lead to an insatiable desire for recognition. They need to be seen as "the person who did all of this for you."

The "low love and low guilt" people always assume they know what is best for the other person. They do not understand that a lecture on drowning is of no help to a person going under for the third time. These strong individualists are often impatient with the weaknesses they see in others.

Emotionally driven Christians may sacrifice more for faraway places and at the same time possess a callous unconcern for the nearby person next door. This contradiction in behavior is because of an unrecognized self-concern. "What loving thing can I do to make me feel better?" They would join the Judgment Day chorus, "Lord, when saw we thee an hungred, or athirst . . . and did not minister unto thee?" (Matt. 25:44). They are so concerned about themselves, they do not see the needs at hand, only those at a safe distance.

It is possible to be loving persons and not feel guilty. Love does not need to be motivated by guilt. Loving persons may see a need, analyze their relationship to it, and make a decision to volunteer their help without feeling great positive or negative emotion in the process. Their motivation for volunteering will continue as long as the needs exist.

Guilt motivates people for the short run but never the long run. People who are motivated by guilt will not last long on the job. When they no longer feel guilty, they no longer feel motivated. As a motivator, guilt works, but not for long.

Guilt works with some people but not with others. Also, guilt does not work all the time, even with people who are subject to its motivations. When guilt fails to motivate, the tendency is to ratchet up the level of guilt and invest the situation with more emotion. In summary: Guilt will work with some people in some situations when the needs of the potential volunteer happen to match the needs or the challenge of the moment.

The loving people make the best volunteers. They can visualize the need and see a clear picture of what can reasonably be done. Their level of volunteering will not rise and fall with their feelings.

The results of this study indicate that guilt does not maintain consistent helping behavior because it inhibits a person's ability to accurately perceive the need of others. The persons with a heavy load of guilt are wearing a set of glasses with mirrors on the inside. When they look out on the needs of others, what they really see is themselves, mired down in their own troublesome feeling of guilt. If volunteering money, time, energy, or skill will alleviate the guilt, then you can count on them to volunteer.

Church members who value wisdom, creativity, or skill more than they value becoming a loving person themselves do not necessarily feel guilty. They just have a different set of values. The concern of the strong individualist is focused on effectiveness and achievement, not on feelings of love.

The final observation in this study, and one of the most important ones, is that love can be learned. It is not a chemical substance in the genes, but rather a learned response. It is a way of looking at life. Parents teach children to love, and long-term pastors can, within limits, teach congregations to be loving and supportive of one another.

Jesus was the ultimate Volunteer. (1) He was love personified, although He seldom wept in public. (2) His love was unconditional. He poured out His love on people who did not deserve it. (3) His love was selfless. His vision was not distorted—blinders never narrowed His vision, and mirrors never reflected love back on himself. He loved sinners and innocent children alike. He never healed anyone for show. In love, He was meeting the needs of others, not His own. And, (4) His love was pure from guilt. Try as they might, by their false accusations, the scribes could not make Him feel guilty, not even on minute matters of Sabbath observance.

If Christ by His power can save us from the state of guilt that separates us from God and otherwise drives us into the ultimate hell of eternal separation from Him, then He can by His presence teach us how to live free from the horrors of self-imposed guilt.

No one raises his children perfectly. Therefore, we can feel guilty about it or do the best we can and then put them into the hands of God. No one minds his social manners perfectly. Therefore, we can feel guilty or do the best we know how and put the results into the hands of God. Paul said, "Forgetting those things which are behind, . . . I press toward the mark" (Phil. 3:13-14).

Love without guilt is not a static state. It is a process, a lifelong process. We will never be perfect persons in this life. There are too many ways to fail. But we can learn to keep our faults and failures on the altar of His love. We can learn to sing "Just as I Am" as an ode to Christian joy as well as an invitation to sinners in a state of guilt.

8

Creating the Atmosphere

For many people, the atmosphere in a church is almost as important as their theology. There was a time when families joined a church for life, but not anymore. When people move from one town to another, they often look for a church with the kind of atmosphere they like, whether or not it has a familiar name over the door. When people only move across town, the occasion is often used to hunt for a church with a better atmosphere than the one they belonged to in the old neighborhood. Fewer families focus their search today on theological considerations as their parents and grandparents did. What most people seem to want is an atmosphere they describe as friendly, spiritual, and accepting.

Most of us know people who have left the theological certitudes of the Church of the Nazarene for what they experience as the more hospitable atmosphere of a charismatic congregation, a Calvinistic church, or the free spirit of a nondenominational group. If theology were a fact at all in their membership transfers, it was, at least, secondary. They moved into what they perceived to be a more hospitable atmosphere, away from one they felt was cold, unfriendly, unspiritual, or strident.

We Nazarenes have also seen moves work the other direction with families who have seemingly made an easy transition from a church with another theological tradition into ours because they saw the local Nazarene congregation as happy, free, loving, and warm.

This same concern for the good atmosphere affects the motivations of volunteers. Some people sit uninvolved in one church, yet on moving into the new atmosphere of a different congregation, they become volunteers, using physical and spiritual energies that had lain dormant. Sometimes, a shift in leadership will change the atmosphere in a local church, so that former bystanders suddenly get involved.

This impact of atmosphere on behavior is seen in many ways. In outer space bodies are free-floating, while the same bodies within the earth's gravitational pull are drawn downward in keeping with Newton's law of gravity. The atmosphere for motivating education in the ghetto is altogether different than academic motivation of an upper middle class neighborhood. Motivations for living with Christian values are altogether different on the campus of a Christian college than they are in a highly secular, Ivy League school. Since we tend to behave like we dress, a wedding gown or a bathing suit will signal different patterns of behavior because of the self-atmosphere the clothes generate.

There are some equally important differences between the impact of potential Christian volunteers in one church contrasted to similar people in another. These differences seem to focus on such things as (1) quality of leadership, (2) a sense of mission, and (3) organizational planning. The pastor and congregation who create a good atmosphere for volunteers will be greatly rewarded. The church that is (1) legalistic, (2) negative, and (3) dominated by one strong family who is negative or legalistic will find it almost impossible to motivate people to volunteer because the atmosphere is wrong.

QUALITY OF LEADERSHIP

Years ago when Edward Lawlor was a highly successful pastor in Calgary, Alta., and I was in the beginning stage of my ministry, he invited me to preach in his church on a Sunday evening. I was more impressed than I had ever been with any church I had ever experienced. The big choir sang as if they were inspired. All the seats in the main sanctuary were taken plus a full balcony. The platform was beautifully decorated with flowers and palms. The organist played with authority as did the highly gifted pianist. The ushers moved about as if they knew what they were doing. The offering plates were full. In fact, everything, as I saw it, was impressive and memorable. I had never seen such a Sunday night service. Where I came from, the Sunday night service was a poor man's rerun of the Sunday morning service, just less prepared. In Dr. Lawlor's service, everybody was happy. Everybody sang. And everybody listened with obvious intent. It was easy to preach, and people moved out to the altar readily when the invitation was given.

The next day, while I was following Pastor Lawlor around, trying to learn all I could about being a good pastor, I asked him, "What is the most important thing you do?" Without hesitating to think or decide how to answer me, he replied, "The most important thing I do is to create a radiant atmosphere of happy optimism in the church." Then he went on, "The church will grow in direct ratio to the spirit of radiant, happy optimism that obtains in the congregation."

Suddenly it dawned on me. The factor that made the service outstanding the night before was atmosphere. The usual functions of a Sunday evening service were excellent, but these did not make the service outstanding. All of these standard Sunday evening functions in a church came together under the leadership of a positive pastor who created the atmosphere that motivated people to participate by singing, listening, giving, or whatever else they were called on to do. This was a church full of volunteers because the pastor created a positive atmosphere.

All of the pastors and lay leaders in all the churches in the world can be identified under three categories.

Some leaders are authoritarian. These people function best when they are in total control. In fact, control is all-important. They believe their way of doing things is the best way or maybe the only way. These kinds of leaders do very well in getting things moving, but they do not create an atmosphere that wears well. The spiritual humidity they generate makes for a sticky atmosphere. An authoritarian atmosphere makes volunteers feel uncomfortable and wear out early. Like any atmosphere that is heavy, the fatigue factor is high. Authoritarian leadership makes for two kinds of volunteers: Some people respond to leadership without question, while others experience a high frustration level and tend more and more to resist domination. The final result is usually a blowup.

Other leaders are laissez-faire in their approach to volunteers. They have a hands-off operation, which sometimes comes across as not caring. The volunteers don't feel much responsibility because the leader shows little concern. Personal popularity is more important to the laissez-faire leader than the discipline of results. In this open atmosphere nothing much gets done. But it is hard to oppose the leader because he never takes a stand nor does anything that risks his popularity. This kind of leader keeps the buck moving so that it seldom stops at his desk.

Among volunteers, this laissez-faire atmosphere is usually permeated with mild dissent, which is like a low-grade fever. The atmosphere seldom turns malignant, but it also fails to enjoy the state of good health that motivates volunteers with commitment and enthusiasm.

Other leaders take a democratic approach that involves the people in creating the atmosphere that motivates volunteers. The leader serves as a resource person. The democratic leader talks with the people who will do the work, so everyone buys into the goals and plans. "Participatory democracy" is a buzzword with these kinds of leaders.

Democratic leaders believe strongly in their own ideas and abilities, but they are equally open to the ideas and abilities of others. These leaders wear well. The atmosphere they create endures and makes it easy for people to become effective volunteers over a long span of years.

In the democratic atmosphere there is more interest in developing people than in reaching goals. With these leaders, direction and movement are more important than counting and winning. These leaders are people oriented. They are not driven primarily by numbers or the need for visible success. Their reward is the inner sense of a job well done.

In contrast to the authoritarian leader, whose highest good is personal control, or the laissez-faire leader, whose highest good is his own personal popularity, the democratic leader is someone who has loyal followers because his leadership creates a people atmosphere that is positive, one that motivates volunteers to enjoy their work.

A SENSE OF MISSION

The Christian movement has always been endowed with a sense of mission. When Jesus recruited His first 12 followers, they were called to be fishers of men. When His 70 volunteers spread out across Galilee, their mission was to proclaim the kingdom of God. When Jesus prepared to leave His followers on the Mount of Olives, He gave them the Great Commission: "Go ye into all the world, and preach the gospel to every creature" (Mark 16:15).

Paul's mission was to proclaim the gospel to the Gentiles. He did so with an effectiveness that caused King Agrippa to say, "Almost thou persuadest me" (Acts 26:28).

John's mission was to teach the love of Christ, which he proclaimed faithfully in an Ephesian school until he was almost 100 years old.

Every church where enthusiastic volunteers do their work with commitment is endowed with a sense of mission. The first priority for motivating volunteers is positive leadership by a faithful, good-spirited pastor. The second most important factor in creating the atmosphere for volunteers is a well-defined mission. This mission needs to be clearly stated, widely accepted, and internally believed. The first generation of Christians knew what their mission was. They were to go into all their world, preaching and teaching the gospel, baptizing believers, and gathering them into a church. This mission was translated into operational terms they could follow. Anywhere a Christian family moved, they started a meeting of believers in their own home. And for 300 years, the "house church" was the only kind of church the Christian movement knew.

A theology professor taught me that preparation on any sermon began with an incomplete sentence written across the top of a blank piece of paper: "The purpose of this sermon is . . ." When that sentence was completed, the rest of the sermon tended to fall into place. If that sentence was not completed, the sermon could drift any direction, or in several directions at once. Even a sermon needs a sense of mission before it can become a message.

In later years I learned that a Sunday morning worship service needed a sense of mission. Therefore preparations began with a similar unfinished sentence: "The purpose of this Sunday morning service is . . ." When I was able to finish that sentence to my own satisfaction, the worship plans, including hymns, prayers, scripture, choir number, and the like, all fell into place naturally, each part fitting together with the other parts for a service focused on its purpose.

It was some years later that I learned the absolute importance of clarifying, to my own satisfaction, the mission of my pastoral leadership in a given church at a given time.

In my last pastorate the people were, early on, in a state of confusion. The church was located in a downtown concrete and asphalt jungle. It was obvious to me that it would take more than clever contests and sanctified promotion to overcome the status quo and build a strong, expanding church in our location. We did not have the momentum for a move to a new location, and it would probably have taken most of a decade to effect the transition if we tried.

When I gathered our volunteers together the first time, I drew a line down the center of a chalkboard and asked them to tell me the problems and the possibilities of our church. In minutes the problem side of the board was full, and the possibilities side was blank. In trying to find our possibilities, I suggested the assets of a central downtown location, easy access by freeways, a long heritage as an old First Church, and the entire city as our parish without the restrictions of an eastside or westside neighborhood. But I saw none of these possibilities was getting through. They were unimpressed. So, with some final words of hope and encouragement, I dismissed the meeting.

From that point I entered into days and weeks of prayer and thought. What we needed was a clarification of our purpose. We needed a reason for being. We needed more than the propagation of our heritage, even though the church was founded by Phineas Bresee in 1905.

We needed a mission, one that I could believe in with my whole heart and bleed for, one the people could buy into with enthusiasm. (1) We discussed building a great citywide Sunday School. (2) We talked about a downtown evangelistic center including celebrity events, a great revival spirit, and a focus on public services rather than Sunday School and Christian education. (3) We talked about turning to the immediate neighborhood. After all, a detective who came to examine a church break-in told me the easiest place in town to buy drugs was within a block of our church. And there were certainly enough needy, homeless people to go around.

After much thought, earnest times of prayer, and many long and serious conversations, we completed the unfinished sentence: "The purpose of our church is . . . to build a strong congregation of Christian families." Our mission was to be a family church.

With the mission determined, other things began to fall in place: (1) We canceled the Sunday School bus program and sold the buses. We would work on entire families coming to church together in the family car. (2) We decided there would be something special going on for every member of the family each time they came to church. Even social events would be family events. When we went skating, the whole family went. (3) We organized three children's churches for Sunday morning, set the evening service ahead one hour for the sake of schoolchildren, and declared it a family service complete with a Teen Town, which eventually filled one section of the sanctuary on Sunday nights. Wednesday night prayer meeting was divided into age-groups and special interest groups, more than doubling the attendance in one week. All of this planning came under an unannounced slogan, "If it can't be done on Sunday and Wednesday, it probably can't be done." Our schedule and our programs were set for the purpose and convenience of families.

There is no need for me to go further, for the point is made: After the pastor decides on his mission, many other decisions fall naturally into place. But without a unifying purpose, segments of the church program can actually work against each other. The recruitment of volunteers begins with a clear sense of direction.

THE DILEMMA OF
MAINLINE CHURCHES

From George Washington to George Bush, a small group of mainline churches—Methodist, Episcopal, Presbyterian, and Congregational—have provided the nation with most of its presidents, as well as senators and governors. William McKinney, dean of the Hartford Seminary in Connecticut, believes the "kinder and gentler" America President Bush talked about is a reflection of the values found in these churches, though not exclusive to them.

The once-powerful influence of this mainline group has faded into more than two decades of severe losses in membership. From 1965 to 1987, the Methodists are down 18%, Presbyterians 25%, and Episcopalians 27%.

And in an effort to explain these losses, a report funded by the Lilly Endowment, Inc., in early 1990 said, "These denominations have failed to distinguish their unique message." In other words: They have lost their sense of mission.

Any student of secular business knows a fuzzy sense of mission is the forerunner of failure. When the *Chicago Daily News* went out of business after more than 100 years of service to the city, one of its editorial writers cited the cause as a loss of mission. Sociologist Dean Hoge said the churches in the greatest state of decline are the ones with a "country club atmosphere." They really don't have any mission beyond a superficial social service to each other with a social network that is hard for new people to penetrate. Peter Drucker gives this whole idea of mission its bottom line when he said, "The nonprofit institution exists for the sake of its mission."

Start now to create the climate for volunteering as you clarify the purpose of your church. Unless the pastor and people understand the purpose for the existence of their congregation, it drifts with the winds that blow from the most recent seminars. If you don't know why you are doing what you are doing, it is difficult to resist borrowing patterns and programs from a well-known, growing church whether or not what they are doing fits your situation.

In the last 25 years there have been many evangelical fads that have faded in and out of favor. Each of them met the needs of some churches, but none of them worked profitably for all churches. We copy other churches' programs without understanding their mission and then wonder why their ways don't work for us. Singspirations, bus programs, coffee house ministries, evangelical films, dialogue sermons, celebrity events, and seminar programs are a few of these fads. The singspiration on Sunday nights or the Sunday School bus programs may work effectively in one church and fail miserably in another.

There are multiple reasons why these programs were a success in some places and not in others. But the main reason they failed was the lack of fit with the mission of the church where the transplant was intended to be a new lease on congregational life.

Organization, allocation of resources, investments in time and energy, plus the vast possibilities for mobilizing volunteers begins with a clear statement of the specific purpose of the church.

Peter Drucker, in one of his taped interviews in the series on nonprofit institutions, says, "A mission statement has to be operational or otherwise it is just good intentions." This means the mission statement of the church must focus on what the pastor and congregation are really trying to do. "To win the world for Christ" is too broad a mission because it cannot be put into operational terms. But, "To proclaim Christ to our entire community" is a reasonable goal. If "proclaiming Christ" is the purpose of your church, then certain operational questions follow: How will we proclaim Him? Can we get the people to come into our church to hear Him proclaimed or will we have to go to where they are? And if so, how?

At dinner last night, I asked a layman if he could give me the mission of his church. He didn't hesitate. "Yes," he said. "I think I can. Our mission is to win people to Christ and then educate them so that they, in time, can win others to Christ." Incidentally, the church he attends is growing. In his church, the pastor previews his sermon with a group of volunteers who spend two hours discussing the content and scriptural background of the message. Then these volunteers who have had a thorough baptism into next Sunday morning's sermon become teachers who meet in groups with the teens and adults for a 45-minute discussion following the message. This discussion of the pastor's sermon is their adult Sunday School curriculum.

Here are some guidelines for defining the purpose or mission of your church:

The statement must be plain and easily understood. A one-line statement is best, although amplification of the statement may go to a full paragraph or even a page. But in all cases, keep it simple. It must function like a slogan everyone knows.

The pastor and church leaders must feel the mission keenly and understand it fully. If you borrow a mission statement or create your own, think and pray about it long enough to be sure you believe it fully.

The mission statement must be turned into operational terms. "These are the things we must do to fulfill our purpose." Determine which to make now and when to make the others.

The statement must not be too broad or too narrow. If it is too broad, it cannot be put into operational terms. You can't be all things to all people. If the statement is too narrow, it has no meaning.

At strategic points in the ongoing life of the church, the mission needs to be reviewed and possibly changed or adjusted. This need for review and revision probably comes every five to seven years.

The most important part of implementing a mission statement is to help every volunteer see how his work contributes toward the fulfilling of the church's reason for being. If you are building a family church, it is good to teach nursery attendants, ushers, and all others to think in terms of the family. If your mission is to be an evangelistic church, the focus of everything shifts to evangelism. Being a missionary church, a Christian community center, or a holiness church calls for their own focus of concern.

The most difficult part of implementing a mission statement is the organized abandonment of programs that do not contribute to the fulfillment of the mission and the reallocation of funds and energy to programs that do. Churches have a hard time feeding their strengths and starving their weaknesses. There is a tendency to expect perfection. Therefore we take strengths for granted and concentrate on weaknesses. Among all the programs that contribute to the mission, emphasize those that are done best and eliminate the weaker ones by organized abandonment. The idea that every church is good at everything is simply not so. Don't try to do what the Lord has not called you to do.

Seek to discover existing needs that fit your mission and can be matched to your resources in money, facilities, and people. I have clipped a sentence from some unknown source and pasted it on the first page of my datebook: "Anything can be done, but not everything." Creating the climate for volunteers begins with a mission statement that makes sense, is believable, and is easily understood. Then we build programs that match our mission and phase out the others.

Scholars have observed that dinosaurs and other huge animals died in the Ice Age because they couldn't cope with the radical changes in climate. Churches cope with radical changes in the cultural climate by keeping their statement of mission up-to-date. Otherwise the preaching of sermons, singing of songs, reading of scriptures, and making of testimonies are just different means for expressing good intentions. Only the church with a sense of mission inspires great numbers of volunteers who stick with their assignments.

CREATING A PLAN
OF ACTION

The third factor in creating the atmosphere that motivates volunteers is planning combined with action. Without action, the best plans are only good intentions. The church that doesn't know where it is headed will never know if it arrives.

Most church reporting systems focus on the past, not the future. We guarantee failure when we set goals without formulating plans on how and when these goals will be reached. "Our church didn't pay the budgets this year, but we intend to next year" is an expression of good intentions and nothing more. If we see signs that "things are beginning to happen in our church," we tend to believe next year will be a better year. But next year will only be a better year if the plans of the church are attached to a time schedule that guarantees attention to well-focused goals.

However, the hoped-for results won't come next year or the year after if the church is drifting on a sea of good intentions. If there are no plans to make next year any different from all the other years, the church will go through all the functions other churches go through, but there will be no forward movement. For lack of a mission and a set of action plans a local church can only struggle to hold its own.

The church with (1) quality leadership in the pastor and among the laymen, and (2) a clearly defined sense of mission, is ready to (3) lay out plans that will accomplish its mission.

Good intentions do not move mountains, bulldozers do. And in churches, volunteers are the bulldozers. Churches who plan to recruit volunteers to move the mountains need well-stated plans the volunteers can follow. Pray for miracles but plan for results. Strategies are the action plans that convert what we want to do into the results we desire.

Once the mission is in mind, it is time for the pastor and the lay leaders to make certain assumptions. For instance, you may assume the possibility of salvation is increased if more people attend church regularly. This is akin to the assumption in education that the boy or girl who sits at the desk regularly will learn more than the one who does not. If you believe this, then begin devising plans to get more people in church on a regular basis. An increased attendance won't happen if you don't plan for it. What do people expect who attend church? William Barclay said he expected to (1) feel something, (2) to be given something to think about, and (3) be challenged by something to do. What do you plan to have happen when people attend your church? What makes your people say, "That was a good service"? What can you do that will make people anticipate good services?

Here is another assumption. It is the pastor's job to build a congregation. That is a fair assumption, which must be followed by a string of questions. What kinds of people do we serve best? Where can we go to find these people? What can the volunteers do to help reach these people? What can the pastor do to make the effort of the volunteers productive in bringing new people to church? What should we do, and what should we not do? Questions like these lay the foundation of a workable plan.

Since all churches want more people and need more money, a good plan calls for the best investment of available funds. As we've discussed, this may mean the abandonment of some programs in favor of those that produce the most results.

Some people see all church programs as religious causes. Dropping a program may appear to be cutting back on service to God. But abandoning some programs in favor of others that bear more fruit is just good stewardship in planning the investment of money, time, and energy by the volunteers.

Peter Drucker said he was in a meeting when a pastor reported that anyone "could build a large congregation in five to seven years if his plans focused on five categories of people: (1) youth, (2) singles, (3) young married, (4) family ministry, and (5) ministry to the elderly." If these are your goals, then develop plans to accomplish them. Volunteers will come out of the woodwork when a well-defined set of plans is fully established and communicated. People will suddenly have new optimism because there is realistic hope the church will move ahead.

Our church had averaged within 5 people of 200 for six years when we decided a broad-based Sunday School was important to our mission of building a large family church. Research had turned up some interesting facts that served our purposes. From the research, we learned that Sunday Schools grow according to the size of the organization. We learned the size of the organizational structure was like a blueprint. If you want a bigger house, draw a blueprint with more rooms. As a result, we laid out a plan to appropriately increase the number of our departments and classes.

From the research we also learned that an increase in square footage was necessary to house an expanded organization. Therefore, we brought in an architect and remodeled our Sunday School space to house the expanded organization with its new classes and departments.

From the research we further learned that a well-focused curriculum was necessary to give significant Sunday School attendance. Therefore, we used public school teachers to work with the pastor in choosing the (a) Bible stories, (b) scripture passages, and (c) memory verses a 12-year-old child should know to be scripturally literate. Further plans included the purchase of media equipment and the integration of the new curriculum into both the Sunday School and the children's churches. Suddenly there was a new reason for children to be in Sunday School regularly. The communication of this plan to the people brought forth all the volunteers we needed. They liked the idea of making 6-year-old children biblically literate by the time they were 12 years old. We had a goal and a plan that worked toward our mission as a family church.

If you are suffering from lack of volunteers, (1) look at the quality of your leadership. (2) Examine the reason your church exists as explained in your mission statement. And, (3) be sure your plans for fulfilling your mission have been fully communicated to the potential volunteers.

This is how the atmosphere is created that motivates volunteers in the local church. Know who you are, where you are going, and why you are doing what you are doing. When you know these things, tell others. The atmosphere will begin to build into one that makes people want to join forces.

9

Why Church Members Volunteer

In John Stott's book *One People,* he laments the fact that in many churches laymen are mainly frozen assets. They are the unemployed in the labor force. If they could only be assigned the right job, they would undergo a metamorphosis like a worm becoming a butterfly. It is the experience of many church leaders that working Christians smile more, look better, enjoy their church more, and are easier to live with than the chronically unemployed.

Church members in a nonproductive state sit passively listening to sermons that often miss their mark. They react unappreciatively to music that has been planned to lift their flagging spirits. They respond with their ears and not their hearts to prayers that feature supplications focused on the complications in their lives. But none of these endeavors, which are standard fare in most worship services, ever serves as the elixir to change their ways.

What church members need is not better sermons, more inspirational music, or more helpful prayers. What unemployed church members need is something to do. And a good job is defined as a work assignment that the worker feels makes a difference. Frustrated uselessness is more dangerous in a church than worldliness. A cadre of useless church members who stay around primarily for the social connections will become the hotbed in which the seeds of a negative spirit are sown. The Halfway Covenant didn't work in the 18th century, and it doesn't work now. The most important challenge the pastor has is to replace the congregation's scandal of uselessness with a great corps of happy volunteers.

God has created every church member with unique and valuable gifts. Some gifts are highly visible, while others are understated and need the cultivation of a good spiritual gardener. The foremost job of the pastor and his team of lay leaders is to (1) discover, (2) develop, and (3) direct the gifts within the membership of the congregation. We need to "equip . . . the saints for . . . service" (Eph. 4:12, NASB).

Each Christian has a mission in the world. In Paul's letters to the Romans and again in his correspondence with the Corinthians, he reminded his readers they were "called to be saints" (Rom. 1:7; 1 Cor. 1:2). God has called us out of the world that He may send us back into it. And for most of us, that means service through our local church, with a pastor to guide us, and a lay group to encourage us.

This call of God is nontransferable. No other Christian can do what you or I are called to do. Ministry is the mission of every Christian. If ministry is only for the ordained, we are in trouble, since almost all of the Christians in the world are laymen. Someone estimated, after much figuring, that less than 1% of the Christians in the world are ordained. Therefore, voluntary service must be the responsibility of every believer for whom Christ died.

THE BIBLICAL MANDATE

The most compelling factor in Christian motivation for voluntary service is the biblical mandate. Jesus was the ultimate Volunteer. He gave himself. He poured out His life, absorbing in himself all the sins of the world. But in His pilgrimage, which ultimately led Him to Calvary, He lived and worked with volunteers. On one occasion He recruited 70 volunteers to cover Galilee with the message of the kingdom of God. The bulk of His ministry was absorbed in the training of the apostles whom He had recruited. Jesus never hesitated to draft volunteers. He sent volunteers to fetch the donkey He would ride into Jerusalem. Other volunteers made arrangements for the loan or rental of the Upper Room. Volunteers filled the empty pots at the wedding in Cana.

The voluntary service of the disciples was not without failures. Peter fell asleep in Gethsemane when Jesus needed him most. One of His volunteers, Judas, turned against Him as the catalyst for setting up for His arrest, trial, and death. Some quarreled over the importance of their assignments. They even got their families involved. All of them misunderstood His mission. But Jesus kept working with imperfect volunteers, saving His strength and energy for the specific things the Father had sent Him to do—things like healing and the forgiveness of sinners. But through all His ministry, Jesus leaned heavily on the work of the volunteers.

Paul included volunteerism in the curriculum of young ministers. His most-prized student, Timothy, got the message: "And the things you have heard me say . . . entrust to reliable men who will also be qualified to teach others" (2 Tim. 2:2, NIV). Paul expanded this admonition for developing volunteers from leaders to the whole congregation when he commissioned the Ephesian congregation "for the perfecting of the saints, for the work of the ministry, for the edifying of the body of Christ" (Eph. 4:12).

Moses, the leader of God's chosen people, became the great Old Testament example of the man who organized his entire assignment through volunteers. He who started out trying to do everything himself became the foremost Old

Testament example of organizing great amounts of work in manageable proportions through volunteers.

Moses' servant of light was his father-in-law, Jethro, who taught him to inspire volunteers who had been there all the time, but no one had asked for their help. He said, "The thing that you are doing is not good. You will surely wear out, both yourself and these people who are with you, for the task is too heavy for you; you cannot do it alone" (Exod. 18:17-18, NASB).

Moses listened to his father-in-law and began the task of recruiting thousands of volunteers who would accept responsibility. Each supervisor was trained to supervise and care for the needs of a small group. There were large numbers to care for an estimated 3 million men, women, and children. But their needs were met in small groups led by a volunteer.

The success of this system of voluntary service cannot be assailed. The people survived their ordeal in the desert. Moses escaped a physical or emotional break and lived to be an old man whose strength was not abated at 120 years of age (Deut. 34:7). If Moses had not listened to his father-in-law, Jethro, he might well have become one more sidetracked leader who was burned out ahead of his time. And certainly, he would have been one more leader who primarily gave himself to the daily routine while he missed the things that were really important. In Moses' case, the important work included the leadership of God's people, receiving the Ten Commandments, establishing the Tabernacle for worship, and teaching faith in the one true God, Jehovah. The threat to Moses' leadership was the tyranny of the daily routine, which, fortunately, he learned to share with a loyal cadre of faithful volunteers.

Reviewing the biblical mandate for a volunteer ministry leaves us with some updated suggestions for church leaders: (1) Through Christ we can do all things, but not everything. (2) Trying to do everything sets a low ceiling on the capacity of the leader to achieve important purposes. (3)

Irritability, chronic fatigue, and self-pity are the first signs of burnout. (4) The leader who tries to do everything goes to bed feeling guilty because church work, by its very nature, is never finished. It is never possible to get everything done by the end of any given day.

WHEN THE SITUATION
IS SATISFACTORY

Experienced church leaders know church members volunteer more happily when the working situation is satisfactory. Volunteers look at the need and test it against their own skills and interests. They look to see with whom they will be working and test those potential relationships against their own past experiences of working with similar people. They study the working environment to see if space and equipment meet acceptable standards. They look at the time requirements and test them against their own schedules and the amount of time and energy they are able and willing to give. The situation is satisfactory when most of these factors come together in a positive way. If the prospective volunteer does not like the people involved, feels the time demands are unreasonable, and the required skills are beyond their ability to perform, then the likelihood of being motivated by a satisfactory situation is greatly reduced.

Michael Phillips of Fordham University did a study that illustrates this concept of need for a satisfactory situation ("Motivation and Expectation in Successful Volunteerism"). His study evaluated the motivations of families in 321 communities nationwide who accepted 1 or more of the 11,000 children from deprived homes in New York City for a two-week summer break.

To begin with, the idea of hosting a child is altruistic and appeals to love and concern for the less fortunate. However, the probable downside of stress and strain on the family also enters the decision process. The family begins to face the probable costs in money, time, relationships, and the like. Self-interest raises its head. How much will they enjoy the presence of the child? What are the benefits of exposure to a child from another culture whose behavior has developed out of a radically different life-style and value system? The family may test their concerns on friends and relatives to get their reactions. At this point they are looking for emotional support for their potential volunteering. They may try to reduce the risks in the unknown by requesting a child in a certain age range and of a certain ethnic background.

When the child arrives, the dynamics of the child's expectations and the family's expectations come into play. A breakdown on either side can be ruinous to the voluntary process. The situation must be satisfactory. A good experience will reinforce the commitment of the family to volunteer again the next year. This means the cost the family was willing to pay in personal adjustment to schedules, investment of time, and expenditure of energy were met or exceeded by the satisfactions of the two-week experience.

Although most church volunteers have strong biblical, theological, and spiritual reasons for volunteering their services to Christ and His Church, every church member is still a human being who will, someplace in the process, stop to examine the returns on his voluntary effort. This is human, not carnal.

The original loving concern of the volunteer is reinforced, sustained, and eventually established as a long-term relationship if the family perceives the effort is worth the cost. If the situation is not satisfactory, there are many other needs and causes calling for volunteer solutions that at the same time afford a more commensurate amount of personal satisfaction.

Sometimes, the matter of a satisfactory situation becomes more important in keeping volunteers than in recruiting them. Virginia Patterson studied the motivational factors among women who served as club leaders in evangelical churches, for her doctoral dissertation at Northern Illinois University. The four strongest motivational factors at time of recruitment were (1) the opportunity to serve, (2) strong belief in the program, (3) involvement with other women, and (4) the possibility of a learning and growing situation.

However, the reason women gave for continuing their voluntary service as club leaders was not the same they gave for volunteering in the first place. An opportunity to serve, which was the foremost motivational factor in the beginning, gave way to a deeper motivation that was based on a satisfactory situation. The women who stayed with their assignments on the long pull reported strong positive feelings about the results of the program and their personal efforts in it. They had a continuing desire to serve because the situation had proven to be satisfactory.

THE CALL OF GOD

There is a great amount of literature on the subject of motivating volunteers. However, most of it is based on the humanistic principles laid down in the scholarly work of men like Gordon Allport, Carl Rogers, and Abraham Maslow, titans in the field of social science. These men can explain motivation in humanistic terms, ignoring a human's connection to his Maker or a person's inborn sense of responsibility to their neighbor. They see volunteerism as a window of light on the fulfillment or actualization of the self. Unfortunately, much of the evangelical literature on motivation of volunteers is written from the humanistic perspective.

In every congregation, there are people who volunteer themselves because they have felt the call of God. These are the people to watch. The usual categories of motivational theory do not apply to them. They hear the sound of a trumpet others have not caught. They march to a drumbeat that comes in on a spiritual frequency beyond the hearing of most mortals. These are the people who often transcend the usual levels of motivation for volunteering to become lay ministers. They may not be ordained as persons, but their ministry is ordained.

The Sunday School Board of the Southern Baptist Convention did a study to determine why people volunteered in Baptist churches. They surveyed 11,458 volunteers from 427 churches with an average of 29 volunteers per church.

The top three reasons given by Baptists for volunteering in their local church run counter to the usual results reported by social scientists. Their results did not support the self-actualization assumptions that have prevailed in most secular research. The top three reasons given by Baptists for volunteering were (1) "I felt God's call to this work." (2) "I wanted to help others learn of God, Christ, the Holy Spirit, and the Bible." And (3) "It is my obligation to witness and spread the gospel."

Reginald M. McDonough, who reported this study, did express concern over the proportion of these Baptists who were motivated out of love for God and those who were motivated from fear of Him because of their guilt. "To love people," he said, "and want to help them is certainly a worthy, Christlike motive. However, some persons want to help others out of their sense of guilt . . . these people may feel God will punish them if they do not serve others." As the humanists strive for self-actualization, Christians may strive toward spiritual actualization through a love for Christ that is free of guilt.

Wayne Michael Worthley, in a doctoral dissertation at the University of Oregon, determined that fundamentalist church volunteers reflected higher spiritual concerns than Sunday School volunteers in liberal churches who demonstrated more social concerns. Other studies have supported his findings. Volunteers who have heard the call of God tend to come from conservative churches.

The hierarchy of human need in the self-actualization approach is based on the assumption that each level of human need must be met before a person is ready to respond to the next-higher level of motivation. The theory, which was developed and widely written on by Abraham Maslow, goes as follows:

1. The lowest level of human need is the need to survive. A man who is struggling with the waves to keep from drowning is not susceptible to a pitch on the four spiritual laws. This is one of the reasons medical missions is important in Third World countries. The need to survive comes first in the hierarchy of human needs.

2. The second level of human need is for security. After the man has been saved from drowning, he is concerned about getting far enough from the water to keep himself secure from any future threat to his survival. After the hungry man has been satisfied with a bountiful meal, his interests shift toward the security that comes with confidence that subsequent meals will be reliably available as needed.

3. The person who has survived and feels secure is now interested in the need to be loved and appreciated. However, these social needs have no power over the person who is striving to survive or is threatened by insecurity. The hostage is concerned about survival and security. But once released and assimilated back into the cultural mainstream, love and affection become meaningful priorities.

4. The fourth hierarchy of human need is for achievement and recognition of this achievement. The worker who has secured his job may become interested in how he can gain the respect of his colleagues and superiors. He may strive for a promotion or a raise.

5. And finally, according to Maslow, the highest level in the hierarchy is the need for self-actualization. Abraham Lincoln, General Eisenhower, and Mother Teresa are examples of people who seem to have grown to their full human potential. They have become what they were intended to become.

Against this backdrop in hierarchies of human need, I suggest there are levels of motivation among church volunteers. If so, let me suggest the following scheme:

1. The lowest level of motivation in a local church is competition. This is the reds against the blues. Competition appeals to a basic human urge, which is to defend one's territory. The principle works in football, but it is not the best motivation for Christ's work on earth. It will bring immediate results in some situations, but the results are short-lived and subject to controversy over the rules for tabulating the score.

2. The next level in motivating church members to volunteer is recognition and approval. The congregation that develops its level of voluntary service on the frequency and amount of public stroking of volunteers is subject to great swings in the highs and lows of self-worth. This kind of motivation appeals probably to a higher source within us than competition, but just barely.

3. The third level of voluntary services is motivation by guilt. Guilt motivation is effective with many church-goers. And most pastors know it. "If I can make the people feel guilty, then I can get them to respond." There is one basic problem in motivation by guilt: As soon as the person with guilt feelings volunteers, their motivation level begins to drop. They don't feel guilty, as they did before they volunteered. After a short while they do not feel guilty at all, and the irresistible temptation to drop out looms large. Another problem with motivation by guilt is the heavy dependency on emotion in the decision. The result is erratic bursts of volunteering because the emotion of guilt rises and falls on easy provocation. However, with all its faults, guilt is the most widely used tool in motivating church people to volunteer their time and money.

4. Commitment to meeting a need is the next level of motivation in the local church. The person who is motivated by a clear vision of a need they can fill may say: "I do not give this cup of cold water to make me feel better. I give it because there are thirsty people whom I can serve." They sing in the choir because the church needs people to sing in the choir and they can sing. They give because the

church needs money and they have money to give. They do not ask, "How am I doing?" but, "How are they doing?"

5. The ultimate spiritual fulfillment comes in lay ministry. Paul served people because the love of Christ constrained him. Local church volunteers who have caught the vision to fulfil their lives through a lay ministry are spiritually actualized. They no longer say, "Let me serve You, O God, but in an advisory capacity." They have joined the Isaiahs of the world in saying, "Here am I; send me" (Isa. 6:8).

ROBERT FARRAR'S STUDY

The most useful dissertation I have read on why people volunteer in local churches was done by Robert Farrar at the University of Houston. The volunteers in his study were members of the Methodist, Baptist, Lutheran, and Disciples of Christ churches in Kingwood, Tex., a suburb of Houston, 30 minutes from downtown.

Farrar's study focused on four questions: (1) Why do people volunteer in church? (2) How satisfied are the volunteers in local churches? (3) Why do some church volunteers quit? And, (4) why do some church members never volunteer? These are four questions that must surely strike a responsive chord within pastors and lay leaders who depend on volunteers.

Farrar distributed 1,000 study forms to the volunteers and nonvolunteers in these four churches. After analyzing his data, Farrar came up with some interesting and reassuring information. The reasons church members do, or do not, volunteer are clearly defined.

1. Why do church members volunteer?

The number one reason people gave for doing volunteer work in their local church was their faith, or theology. They said, "I want to put my faith to work in a meaningful way." They saw working in the church as "an opportunity to express my gratitude to God through service in the church."

A close second to faith and theology as motivating reasons for volunteering was a strong love for their local church. For instance: "I am a volunteer in the church because there are significant needs to be met, and the church needs help in meeting them." There was another way of saying the same thing: "I am a volunteer in the church because I want to be part of the program of the church." Therefore, many people volunteer because they love their church, and their church needs help.

2. How satisfied are volunteers in the church?

Farrar found the happiest volunteers talked about their feelings of personal growth and how they were better people because of their involvement in the church. And the second reason volunteers gave for feeling happy about their work in church was the significance of what they were doing.

If you want to keep volunteers for the long pull, be sure they see their work is significant, and be sure their work provides opportunity for personal growth. Repetitive work without significance fosters a high dropout rate among most volunteers.

3. Why do some church volunteers quit?

Farrar's data suggests volunteers drop out when they have sustained feelings that their work didn't make any difference. They quit when they felt their work really didn't matter.

The next most frequent reason for quitting was disappointment with the church staff or lay leaders. The major complaint against staff and other supervisors was the breakdown in communications. Volunteers became distraught when they did not know what was expected of them. And the easiest way for a volunteer to solve a breakdown in communications is to resign.

4. Why do some church members never volunteer?

The number one reason given by church members for not volunteering was too obvious to stumble over: "I have never been asked!" This reason reinforces a story about Mrs.

Marshall Field, who gave $1 million to the University of Chicago but did not give anything to Northwestern University, which was her denominational school. When asked, "Why?" she said, "Northwestern never asked me, and the University of Chicago did." James said, "Ye have not, because ye ask not" (4:2).

Another reason laymen gave for not volunteering was their unwillingness to commit for the long term. This supports the idea that no church assignments should be for more than a year, and many of them should be for less time. People are more willing to enter the tunnel if they can see light at the other end.

However, whatever the reason for quitting, allow volunteers to resign without putting them down, making them feel guilty, or arguing with them over the terrible problem their resignation has created. If you have to pressure people to work in the church, you will have to keep up the pressure to keep them working. And that is self-defeating strategy in motivating Christian volunteers.

Although no mention was made in Farrar's study, the need to prepare people for their assignments and offer them in-service training is important in keeping good people. Willingness to serve does not guarantee quality of service. It is not enough to fill job slots in the church. The local church needs quality people with adequate skills. And technical skills for teaching, singing, or driving the van are heavily discounted if volunteers have trouble working with each other. Very few pastors realize that human relations skills can be taught, but they can. Never leave human understanding out of the curriculum for training volunteers.

There are predictable differences among local churches even within the same denomination. Theological differences may be in matters of focus, emphasis, or degree, but there are theological differences among congregations, as every moving church family knows. There are differences in styles of worship, including preaching, singing, and audience response. There are differences in the proportions of blue collar and white collar workers in each congregation. The age distributions are different from church to church. However, when it comes to volunteering in the local church, the reasons among church members from congregation to congregation are remarkably similar:

1. Church members volunteer because of their gratitude to God, and because they love their local church, which has needs they can help meet.

2. Volunteers lose interest in their church assignments when they feel their work does not make a difference, or when communication problems develop with leadership.

3. Most of the potential volunteers do not sign up because nobody asked them, or they feel the time commitment is unrealistic.

4. A lay ministry obtains when volunteers with skills and commitment transcend competition, need for petty approval, stroking, and guilt, to serve for the constraining love of Christ.

5. The volunteers who learn to work with authority figures without feeling threatened are likely to feel good about themselves and their assignment. Volunteers who are hung up over authority are in for a bumpy ride. In every situation, somebody had to be Chief Indian.

Conclusion: There is ample latent talent in almost every church. It only needs to be discovered, trained, and put to work in the name of Christ and for His sake.

Epilogue
A Theology of Volunteering

Although the biblical mandate on volunteering is plain enough in the Scriptures, the church needs a clearly understood theology of Christian volunteerism.

In the study of voluntary Christian service there are two likely heresies. The first is the tendency toward Christian individualism, which focuses on personal experience without reference to the faith that can only grow in relationships. The second heresy is to explain faith in terms of relationships without the focus on personal salvation, forgiveness, and cleansing in Christ.

Martin Luther Harkey III, in an unpublished doctoral dissertation, says, "Volunteer management principles based on insights from humanistic psychology and management theory have been adapted to the needs of the church, but often without attending to the theological dimensions of volunteering."

Our theologians need to develop a sound and responsible perspective on the ministry of volunteering in the local church. In the absence of an adequate theological statement, and within the obvious limits of my own personal theological understanding, here are some guidelines I feel are important.

Christian service involves what we do with the whole of our lives. The Christian is a whole person, not a schizophrenic, divided between secular and sacred. Christians are persons for whom Christ died. They are persons whose entire lives are a strategy for His glory.

Christian voluntary service is essential in a theology of the church. The call of the believer to a life of service comes under the larger umbrella of the church, which is called to a life of worship and service. You can't have one without the other. Service fulfills the mission of the church.

Motivation, for the believer, should be understood as fulfillment of God's call and not fulfillment of the self. Even the smallest and most lowly task becomes precious service to God when it expresses the faith and gratitude of the believer.

Christian service suggests the believer is not self-contained. The life and work of individual believers is always understood within the context of the church as a gathering of called-out ones whose purpose is worship and service. Voluntary service is involvement in the greater mission of the church.

Christian service is not something to be achieved, but a life to be lived. A life of service is not static. It implies growth. Even when one's life seems futile, it still has eternal significance in God's sight.

A theology of Christian service must also include a study of service in relation to spiritual gifts, the universal priesthood of believers, and Christian servanthood.

In the meantime, I hope this fragmentary look at volunteering in the local church has established the fact that there is a solid theological reason for pastors to lead their people in lives of service, and to give them a biblical reason for continuing involvement in the local church with its eternal sense of Christian mission.

Bibliography

Books

Anderson, James D., and Ezra Earl Jones. *Ministry of the Laity.* San Francisco: Harper and Row, Publishers, 1986.

Bruce, Alexander Balmain, D.D. *The Training of the Twelve, or, Passages out of the Gospels.* New York: George H. Doran Co., 1979.

Christie, Les John. *Unsung Heroes: How to Recruit and Train Volunteer Youth Workers.* Grand Rapids: Zondervan, 1987.

Committee on Aging (U.S.). *Productive Roles in an Older Society.* Washington, D.C.: National Academic Press, 1986.

Conklin, Robert. *How to Get People to Do Things.* Chicago: Contemporary Books, 1979.

Crowe, Jimmy P. *Church Leader Training Handbook.* Rev. ed. Nashville: Convention Press, 1974.

Gallup, George, Jr. *Forecast 2000.* New York: William Morrow and Co., 1984.

Greeley, Andrew M. *The Denominational Society: A Sociological Approach to Religion in America.* Glenview, Ill.: Scott, Foresman and Co., 1972.

Green, Michael. *Called to Serve: Ministry and Ministers in the Church.* Philadelphia: Westminster Press, 1964.

Hall, Calving S., and Gardner Lindzey. *Introduction to Theories of Personality.* New York: John Wiley and Sons, 1985.

Janowitz, Gayle. *Helping Hands: Volunteer Work in Education.* University of Chicago Press, 1966.

Johnson, Douglas W. *The Care and Feeding of Volunteers.* Nashville: Abingdon, 1978.

Kilinski, Kenneth, and Jerry C. Wofford. *Organization and Leadership in the Local Church.* Grand Rapids: Zondervan, 1973.

Klein, Stephen B. *Motivation: Biosocial Approaches.* New York: McGraw-Hill Book Co., 1982.

Lauffer, Armand, and Sarah Gorodesky. *Volunteers.* Beverly Hills, Calif.: Sage, 1977.

Layton, Daphne Niobe. *Philanthropy and Voluntarism: An Annotated Bibliography.* New York: Foundation Center, 1987.

McDonough, Reginald M. *Working with Volunteer Leaders in the Church.* Nashville: Broadman Press, 1976.

McGinnis, Alan Loy. *Bringing Out the Best in People.* Minneapolis: Augsburg Publishing House, 1985.

Menking, Stanley J. *Helping Laity Help Others.* Philadelphia: Westminster Press, 1984.

Moore, Larry F., ed. *Motivating Volunteers: How the Rewards of Unpaid Work Can Meet People's Needs.* Vancouver, B.C.: Vancouver Volunteer Centre, 1985.

Murray, Edward J. *Motivation and Emotion.* London: Prentice-Hall International, 1964.

Newman, Joseph, ed. *People Helping People: U.S. Volunteers in Action.* Washington: Books by U.S. News and World Report, 1971.

O'Connell, Brian. *Effective Leadership in Voluntary Organizations: How to Make the Greatest Use of Citizen Service and Influence.* New York: Association Press, 1986.

———, ed. *America's Voluntary Spirit: A Book of Readings.* New York: Foundation Center, 1983.

Palmer, Bernard. *Pattern for a Total Church*. Wheaton, Ill.: Victor Books, 1975.

Roadcup, David. *Recruiting, Training, and Developing Volunteer Youth Workers*. Cincinnati: Standard Publishing, 1987.

Senter, Mark, III. *The Art of Recruiting Volunteers*. Wheaton, Ill.: Victor Books, 1983.

Stenzel, Anne, and Helen M. Feeney. *Volunteer Training and Development: A Manual for Community Groups*. New York: Seabury Press, 1968.

Stott, John R. W. *One People*. Downers Grove, Ill.: InterVarsity Press, 1968.

Trueblood, Elton. *Your Other Vocation*. New York: Harper and Row, Publishers, 1952.

Vander Zanden, James W. *Social Psychology*. 4th ed. New York: Random House, 1958.

Wilbert, Warren. *Teaching Christian Adults*. Grand Rapids: Baker Book House, 1980.

Wilson, Marlene. *The Effective Management of Volunteer Programs*. Boulder, Colo.: Volunteer Management Assn., 1976.

————. *How to Mobilize Church Volunteers*. Minneapolis: Augsburg Publishing House, 1983.

————. *Survival Skills for Managers*. Boulder, Colo.: Volunteer Management Associates, 1981.

Wurman, Richard Saul. *Information Anxiety*. United States: Doubleday, 1989.

Dissertations

Farrar, Robert Bascom. "Factors Affecting Volunteerism in Church-Related Activities." Copyrighted Ph.D. diss., University of Houston, 1985.

Harkey, Martin Luther, III. "A Theology for the Ministry of Volunteers: with reference to . . . ," Th.D. diss., Southwestern Baptist Seminary, 1985.

Paget, Virginia Marks. "Commitment of Volunteers and the Work of the Church." Ph.D. diss., Washington University, 1982.

Parrott, Leslie, III. "Guilt and Empathy in the Loving Personality." Ph.D. diss., Fuller Theological Seminary, 1988.

Patterson, Virginia C. "Characteristics and Motivational Factors of Volunteer Club Leaders in Evangelical Churches: An Analysis of Pioneer Girls' Club Leaders." Copyrighted Ph.D. diss., Northern Illinois University, 1978.

Rodriquez, Mary Chesley. "A Study and Analysis of the Variables Determining the Retention Behavior of Volunteers." Copyrighted Ph.D. diss., American University, 1983.

Worthley, Wayne Michael. "Factors of Motivation Among Volunteers in the Teaching Ministries Area of Church Christian Education Program: Design of a Teacher Motives Inventory." Ed.D. diss., University of Oregon, 1976.

Articles

Coleman, Joseph. "A Discovery of Commitment." *Annals of the American Academy of Political and Social Science* 365 (May 1966): 12-20.

Connelly, Tom, Jr. "Establishing an Organizational Philosophy: A Cornerstone for Productivity in the Volunteer Organization." *Journal of Volunteer Administration*, Spring 1989, 1-6.

Gillespie, David, and Anthony King. "Demographic Understanding of Volunteerism." *Journal of Sociology and Social Welfare* 12, no. 4 (December 1985): 798-816.

Harder, Ben. "The Student Volunteer Movement for Foreign Missions and Its Contribution to 20th-Century Missions." *Missiology: An International Review* 8, no. 2 (April 1980): 141-54.

Hopkins, C. Howard. "The Legacy of John R. Mott." *International Bulletin of Missionary Research* 5 (April 1981): 70-73.

Howarth, Edgar. "Personality Characteristics of Volunteers." *Psychological Reports* 38 (June 1976): 855-58.

"IS/Gallup Survey Reveals Churches Are Primary Source of Voluntary Aid." *Voluntary Action Leadership,* Winter 1988-89, 5-6.

Karl, Barry D. "Lo, the Poor Volunteer: An Essay on the Relation Between History and Myth." *Social Service Review,* December 1984, 493-522.

Knowles, Malcolm. "Motivation in Volunteerism: Synopsis of a Theory." *Journal of Voluntary Action Research* 1 and 2 (April 1972): 27-29.

Miller, Lynn E. "Understanding the Motivation of Volunteers: An Examination of Personality Differences and Characteristics of Volunteers' Paid Employment." *Journal of Voluntary Action Research* 14 (April—September 1985): 112-22.

Phillips, Michael. "Motivation and Expectation in Successful Volunteerism." *Journal of Voluntary Action Research* 11 (April—September 1982): 118-25.

Robert, Dana L. "The Origin of the Student Volunteer Watchword: The Evangelization of the World in This Generation." *International Bulletin of Missionary Research* 19, no. 4 (October 1986): 146-49.

Smith, Timothy L. "Biblical Ideals in American Christian and Jewish Philanthropy, 1880-1920." *American Jewish History* 74 (1984-85): 3-26.

Stephens, William N. "Contrasting Rewards for Volunteering in Agencies' Programs with Volunteering in Clubs and Churches." *Journal of Volunteer Administration,* Summer 1989, 21-23.

Wiehe, Vernor R., and Lenora Isenhour. "Motivation of Volunteers." *Journal of Social Welfare* 4 (Winter 1977): 73-79.

Paper

Ammons, Edsel A. "Voluntarism and the Church: Implications for Black/White Relation in the United Methodist Church." Copyright by Bureau of Social and Religion Research, 1976. Paper.

Tapes

Drucker, Peter. *The Nonprofit Drucker.* Tyler, Tex.: Leadership Network, 1989.

Wright, Walt. Volunteerism tape recorded in a classroom at Fuller Theological Seminary.